SUSTAINING
PROFESSIONAL
LEARNING
COMMUNITIES

The Soul of Educational Leadership

Alan M. Blankstein, Paul D. Houston, Robert W. Cole, Editors

Volume 1: Engaging EVERY Learner

Volume 2: Out-of-the-Box Leadership

Volume 3: Sustaining Professional Learning Communities

Volume 4: Spirituality in Educational Leadership

Volume 5: Sustainable Leadership Capacity

Volume 6: Leaders as Communicators and Diplomats

Volume 7: Data-Enhanced Leadership

Volume 8: The Schools of Our Dreams

THE SOUL OF EDUCATIONAL LEADERSHIP

VOLUME 3

SUSTAINING PROFESSIONAL LEARNING COMMUNITIES

ALAN M. BLANKSTEIN ◆ PAUL D. HOUSTON ◆ ROBERT W. COLE

EDITORS

A JOINT PUBLICATION

CORWIN PRESS
A SAGE Company
Thousand Oaks, CA 91320

For information:

Corwin Press
A SAGE Company
2455 Teller Road
Thousand Oaks, California 91320
www.corwinpress.com

SAGE Ltd.
1 Oliver's Yard
55 City Road
London EC1Y 1SP
United Kingdom

SAGE India Pvt. Ltd.
B 1/I 1 Mohan Cooperative
    Industrial Area
Mathura Road, New Delhi 110 044
India

SAGE Asia-Pacific
    Pte. Ltd.
33 Pekin Street #02–01
Far East Square
Singapore 048763

Printed in the United States of America

Library of Congress Cataloging-in-Publication Data

Blankstein, Alan M., 1959-
Sustaining professional learning communities / Alan M. Blankstein, Paul D. Houston, Robert W. Cole.
    p. cm.—(Soul of educational leadership series; v. 3)
A joint publication with the HOPE Foundation and the American Association of School Administrators.
Includes bibliographical references and index.
ISBN 978-1-4129-4937-8 (cloth)
ISBN 978-1-4129-4938-5 (pbk.)
    1. School management and organization—United States. 2. Educational leadership—United States. 3. Educational equalization—United States. 4. Academic achievement—United States. I. Houston, Paul D. II. Cole, Robert W., 1945- III. Hope Foundation. IV. Title. V. Series.

LB2801.A2B58 2008
371.2—dc22   2007024754

This book is printed on acid-free paper.

07 08 09 10 11 10 9 8 7 6 5 4 3 2 1

Acquisitions Editor:	Allyson P. Sharp
Editorial Assistant:	David Andrew Gray
Production Editor:	Melanie Birdsall
Copy Editor:	Teresa Herlinger
Typesetter:	C&M Digitals (P) Ltd.
Proofreader:	Gail Fay
Indexer:	Sheila Bodell
Cover Designer:	Michael Dubowe

CONTENTS

ACKNOWLEDGMENTS

W e wish to express our gratitude to those Corwin Press staff members who serve as our lifeline on this project: Allyson Sharp and Lizzie Brenkus, our superb editors; David Gray and Ena Rosen, their on-top-of-everything editorial assistants; and Teresa Herlinger, who catches anything the rest of us miss. Without their unfailingly patient, knowledgeable work, there would be no *The Soul of Educational Leadership* series. All of us are in their debt.

We also wish to express our deepest gratitude to our dozens of contributors. As this series grows in length and breadth, we are humbled by the wealth of deep knowledge and experience brought to this enterprise by dozens of talented, committed educators who have consented to join forces with us. We are merely channeling their life-changing work. Without them, truly this series could not hope to exist.

ABOUT THE EDITORS

Alan M. Blankstein is Founder and President of the HOPE Foundation, a not-for-profit organization whose Honorary Chair is Nobel Prize–winner Archbishop Desmond Tutu. The HOPE Foundation (Harnessing Optimism and Potential through Education) is dedicated to supporting educational leaders over time in creating school cultures where failure is not an option for any student. HOPE has a decade-long track record of sustaining student success in districts throughout North America.

The HOPE Foundation launched the professional learning communities movement in educational circles, first by bringing W. Edwards Deming and his work to light in a series of *Shaping America's Future* forums and PBS video conferences from 1988–1992. Now, the HOPE Foundation provides some 20 conferences annually as well as long-term support for thousands of educational leaders throughout North America and other parts of the world through leadership academies and intensive onsite school change efforts.

A former "high-risk" youth, Alan began his career in education as a music teacher and has worked in youth-serving organizations since 1983, including the March of Dimes; Phi Delta Kappa; and the National Educational Service (now Solution Tree), which he founded in 1987 and directed for 12 years.

Alan is author of the best-selling book *Failure Is Not an Option™: Six Principles That Guide Student Achievement in High-Performing Schools*, which has been awarded "Book of the Year" by the National Staff Development Council. Currently, Alan is Senior Editor along with Paul D. Houston of the eight-volume *The Soul of Educational Leadership* series. Alan also coauthored the *Reaching Today's Youth* curriculum with Rick DuFour and has published articles in *Educational Leadership*, *The School Administrator*, *Executive Educator*, *High School Magazine*, *Reaching Today's Youth*, and

Inside the Workshop. Alan has also given keynote presentations and workshops for virtually every major educational organization.

Alan is on the Harvard International Principals' Center advisory board, has served as a board member for the Federation of Families for Children's Mental Health, is Cochair of Indiana University's Neal Marshall Black Culture Center's Community Network, and is advisor to the Faculty and Staff for Student Excellence (FASE) mentoring program. He is also an advisory board member for the Forum on Race, Equity, and Human Understanding with the Monroe County Schools in Indiana, and served on the Board of Trustees for the Jewish Child Care Agency (JCCA), where he was once a youth-in-residence.

Paul D. Houston has served as Executive Director of the American Association of School Administrators since 1994.

Paul has established himself as one of the leading spokespersons for American education through his extensive speaking engagements, published articles, and regular appearances on national radio and television.

Paul was previously a teacher and building administrator in North Carolina and New Jersey. He has also served as Assistant Superintendent in Birmingham, Alabama, and as Superintendent of Schools in Princeton, New Jersey; Tucson, Arizona; and Riverside, California.

He has also served in an adjunct capacity for the University of North Carolina, Harvard University, Brigham Young University, and Princeton University. In addition, he has worked as a consultant and speaker throughout the United States and overseas, and he has published more than 100 articles in professional journals.

Robert W. Cole is Proprietor and Founder of Edu-Data, a firm specializing in writing, research, and publication services. He was a member of the staff of *Phi Delta Kappan* magazine for 14 years: Assistant Editor from 1974–1976, Managing Editor from 1976–1980, and Editor-in-Chief from 1981–1988. During his tenure as Editor-in-Chief, the *Kappan* earned more than 40 Distinguished Achievement Awards from the Association of Educational Publishers, three of them for his editorials.

Since leaving the *Kappan*, Bob has served as founding Vice President of the Schlechty Center for Leadership in School Reform

(CLSR; 1990–1994). At CLSR, he managed district- and community-wide school reform efforts and led the team that created the Kentucky Superintendents' Leadership Institute. He formed the Bluegrass Leadership Network, in which superintendents worked together to use current leadership concepts to solve reform-oriented management and leadership problems.

As senior consultant to the National Reading Styles Institute (1994–2005), Bob served as editor and lead writer of the Power Reading Program. He and a team of writers and illustrators created a series of hundreds of graded short stories, short novels, and comic books from primer through Grade 10. Those stories were then recorded by Bob and Dr. Marie Carbo; they are being used by schools all across the United States to teach struggling readers.

Bob has served as a Book Development Editor for the Association for Supervision and Curriculum Development (ASCD), for Corwin Press, and for Writer's Edge Press. He has been President of the Educational Press Association of America and member of the EdPress Board of Directors. He has presented workshops, master classes, and lectures at universities nationwide, including at Harvard University, Stanford University, Indiana University, Xavier University, Boise State University, and the University of Southern Maine. He has worked as a special consultant to college and university deans in working with faculties on writing for professional publication. Recently, he began serving as Managing Editor and a senior associate with the Center for Empowered Leadership.

ABOUT THE CONTRIBUTORS

Joseph Aguerrebere is President and CEO of the National Board for Professional Teaching Standards (NBPTS) in Arlington, Virginia. NBPTS is an independent, nonprofit organization that advances quality teaching and learning in American schools by establishing and maintaining professional standards and rigorous performance assessments for what accomplished teachers should know and be able to do. Born and raised in East Los Angeles, Dr. Aguerrebere graduated from the University of Southern California with a bachelor's degree in political science, and master's and doctorate degrees in educational administration. His education career includes serving as a teacher and administrator in elementary, middle, high school, and central office settings in California. He later served as a professor of educational administration at California State University, Dominguez Hills, where he prepared educators to work successfully in urban settings. Prior to joining NBPTS, he was Deputy Director at the Ford Foundation in New York where he supported systemic initiatives to improve the effectiveness of professional educators. He is recognized as a national expert on school reform, serves on numerous boards, and is an advisor to educational organizations, journalists, and government.

Maurice J. Elias is Professor and Coordinator of the Internship Program in Applied, School, and Community Psychology in the Psychology Department, Rutgers University; Director of the Rutgers Social-Emotional Learning Lab and the Developing Safe and Civil Schools (DSACS) prevention initiative (www.rci.rutgers.edu/~melias); and founding member of the Leadership Team for the Collaborative for Academic, Social, and Emotional Learning (www.CASEL.org). Among his writings are *Emotionally Intelligent Parenting* (2000); *Raising*

Emotionally Intelligent Teenagers (2002); *Engaging the Resistant Child Through Computers* (2002); *Building Learning Communities With Character: How to Integrate Academic, Social, and Emotional Learning* (2002); *EQ + IQ = Best Leadership Practices for Caring and Successful Schools* (Corwin Press, 2003); *Bullying, Peer Harassment, and Victimization in the Schools: The Next Generation of Prevention* (2003); *Social Decision Making/Social Problem Solving Curricula for Elementary and Middle School Students* (2006); and *The Educator's Guide to Emotional Intelligence and Academic Achievement: Social-Emotional Learning in the Classroom* (Corwin Press, 2006). Dr. Elias is a licensed psychologist and an approved provider of professional development for educators in New Jersey. He is married and the father of two children.

Andy Hargreaves is the Thomas More Brennan Chair in Education at the Lynch School of Education, Boston College. Prior to that, he was Professor of Educational Leadership and Change at the University of Nottingham, England, and Codirector of and Professor in the International Centre for Educational Change at the Ontario Institute for Studies in Education at the University of Toronto. He is the author and editor of more than 20 books in the fields of teacher development, the culture of the school, and educational reform. Dr. Hargreaves' book *Changing Teachers, Changing Times* received the 1995 Outstanding Writing Award from the American Association of Colleges for Teacher Education, while his 2003 book *Teaching in the Knowledge Society* received outstanding writing awards from the American Educational Association and the American Libraries Association. His most recent book, coauthored with Dean Fink, is *Sustainable Leadership* (2006).

Stephanie A. Hirsh is the Executive Director of the National Staff Development Council. Her primary responsibility includes advancing the council's goal and strategic priorities. In the past several years, her work has focused on helping states, national and state organizations, and selected school systems to develop policies and programs to advance quality professional learning. She facilitated the process that led to the national dissemination of *NSDC's Standards for Staff Development* and *Moving Standards Into Practice: Innovation Configurations*. Dr. Hirsh has been recognized by the Texas Staff Development Council with a Lifetime Achievement Award; by the University of North Texas as a Distinguished Alumnae; and by the Texas Association of School Boards as a Master Trustee. She serves on advisory boards for the Institute for Education Leadership, Microsoft Partners in Learning, Measured Progress, the National Center for Culturally Responsive Education, The University of Texas College of Education Foundation, and The University of North Texas Jewish Studies Program. She has contributed to state policy reform efforts in New Jersey, Ohio, Texas, Missouri, Maryland, North Carolina, and West Virginia, and for the U.S. Department of Education. In addition, she served 9 years as a school board trustee for the Richardson Independent School District (Dallas, TX). Prior to her position with the council, Dr. Hirsh served 15 years in district and school-based leadership positions including public school teacher, community college teacher, consulting teacher for free enterprise, and program and staff development director. Stephanie is married to Mike and they have two children: Brian, 24, and Leslie, 21.

Shirley M. Hord is Scholar Emerita at the Southwest Educational Development Laboratory (SEDL) in Austin, Texas, where she directed the Strategies for Increasing Student Success Program; she continues to monitor the Leadership for Change Project, and to support applications of the Concerns-Based Adoption Model (CBAM). In addition, she designs and coordinates professional development activities related to educational change, school improvement, and school leadership. She served as coordinator of Demonstration Schools, a multi-year rural school improvement project in SEDL's region. Her early roles as elementary school classroom teacher and university science education faculty at The University of Texas at Austin were followed by her appointment at the same school as Codirector of Research on the Improvement Process at the Research and Development Center for Teacher Education. There she administered and conducted research on school improvement and the role of school leadership in school change. Shirley served as a Fellow of the National Center for Effective Schools Research and Development, and was U.S. representative to the Foundation for the International School Improvement Project, an international effort that develops research, training, and policy initiatives to support local school improvement practices. In addition to working with educators at all levels across the United States, Mexico, and Canada, Dr. Hord gives presentations and consults in Asia, Europe, Australia, and Africa.

Larry Leverett, Executive Director of Panasonic Education Foundation, leads a national foundation that supports long-term partnerships with urban school districts across America. Dr. Leverett's career in public education has provided him opportunities to work as a teacher, principal, central office curriculum leader, school board member, superintendent, and assistant commissioner for the New Jersey Department of Education. He is a passionate leader with a deep commitment to equity and social justice. His work has included experiences in both urban and suburban districts. Larry's work with distributed leadership teams resulted in the establishment of linkages between academic achievement and social and emotional learning. He received a BA in elementary education from Virginia State University and an MA and EdD in educational leadership from Teachers College, Columbia University. Dr. Leverett serves on numerous boards including Educators for Social Responsibility, the George Lucas Foundation National Advisory Board, and the advisory committee for the Laura Bush Foundation for School Libraries.

Karen Seashore Louis is Rodney S. Wallace Professor in Educational Policy and Administration at the University of Minnesota. Over the last 30 years, her work has focused on school improvement, and touches on issues ranging from teachers' work to how state policies affect districts and schools. She has been active in national professional organizations, including serving as a vice president of the American Educational Research Association, and on the executive council of the University Council for Educational Administration. She has won a number of awards for her research, including the William J. Davis Award for the best article in the *Educational Administration Quarterly* in 1986 and 1999, and the Paula Silver Award for the best teaching case in 1999. In 1995, she was awarded a Fulbright Fellowship. Karen is currently involved in a study of the effects of leadership on student learning at state, district, and school levels, and in a study of the emergence of distributed leadership in high schools.

Nancy Shin Pascal, more than 30 years ago, began her lifelong career of service teaching junior high French. She subsequently served as a social worker and an analyst for GTE before returning to education in 1989, as Executive Director of the HOPE Foundation. In that capacity, Nancy leads the long-term professional development services of the foundation in 15 states, Canada, and the Hopi Nation. Her work has consistently led to increases in student achievement on standardized tests across geographies, race, and economic status. Over the last 2 years, Nancy has used the *Failure Is Not an Option*

Professional Learning Communities of HOPE approach in urban Milwaukee and in the poorest county in California. In both cases, student proficiency levels have increased substantially. Nancy has helped create award-winning publications and video programs including *Reclaiming Youth at Risk, Discipline With Dignity, Reconnecting Youth,* and *Professional Learning Communities at Work* by Rick DuFour and Bob Eaker. She has coproduced PBS and C-SPAN productions on *Breaking the Cycle of Violence,* as well as *Creating Learning Organizations* with Peter Senge and Dr. W. Edwards Deming. She also has directed professional development for upward of 30,000 educators annually. In addition, Nancy serves as a reviewer for the North Central Regional Educational Laboratory. Nancy's dedication to helping leaders assure success for all children has included serving as an FASE (Faculty And Students for Excellence) mentor at Indiana University and fundraising for international mission work. Nancy has two successful grown children, who now reside on opposite coasts of the United States.

James B. Vetter is Director of Programs of the Open Circle Social Competency Program (www.open-circle.org). Since 1987, Open Circle has provided social and emotional learning curricula and training programs to more than 7,000 teachers as well as hundreds of administrators and other school staff. As a result, the program has reached over 500,000 students in public, private, parochial, urban, suburban, and rural elementary schools in New England and New Jersey. Open Circle is recognized nationally as a science-based program with evidence of effectiveness, having been selected by the U.S. Department of Education's Expert Panel on Safe, Disciplined, and Drug-Free Schools. Open Circle also has been chosen by the Collaborative for Academic, Social, and Emotional Learning (CASEL) as a "CASEL Select Program." Before joining Open Circle, Vetter worked as a violence prevention and conflict resolution specialist, supporting schools and school systems in selecting, implementing, and sustaining science-based social development and youth violence prevention programs. He also developed statewide suicide prevention and youth violence prevention programs for the Virginia Department of Heath. A 1981 graduate of Yale University, Vetter received a master's in education from the Harvard Graduate School of Education, where his studies focused on the sustainability of school-based social and emotional learning programs. He is coauthor of a recent article on the links between violence and suicide that appeared in the journal *Aggression and Violent Behavior.*

Deborah L. Wortham is an area academic officer and a professional educator with 35 years of experience in planning, implementing, and leadership of quality educational programs that meet broad-based student needs. Her assets include excellent leadership and management skills in combination with an understanding of the importance of school culture in the attainment of educational goals and objectives, and commitment to the philosophy of a "Professional Learning Community." She has served as a teacher (selected Teacher of the Year), specialist, assistant principal, principal, and director. Her career highlights include program development and assessment, site-based management and school finance, restructuring models/school improvement and reform, professional development, program evaluation, parent-community relations, and creating professional learning communities. Dr. Wortham received a bachelor's degree in elementary education from the University of Wisconsin, a master's in reading from Morgan State University, and a doctorate in educational leadership from Nova Southeastern University.

INTRODUCTION

ROBERT W. COLE

The profession of education includes both unique rewards and trying sacrifices. The nature of education—preparing young people for life—calls on the hearts, the minds, and the souls of those who work in schools and those who serve as leaders. The title of this multivolume series, *The Soul of Educational Leadership,* signals the deep work demanded of all who have committed their lives to children. From the beginning of this series, we have aimed to seek out contributions from leading thinkers and practitioners on the soul-work of educational leadership.

The theme of Volume 1, *Engaging EVERY Learner,* was selected to signal that every student matters deeply, to all of us in school and in our society. That theme was sounded by Alan M. Blankstein—editor of this series, together with myself and Paul D. Houston: "Saving young people from failure in school is equivalent to saving their lives!" Those powerful words set the tone for all that we hope to do in this series. We know how to do what needs doing, and we are enlisting the thinking of those who have led the way.

In Volume 2, *Out-of-the-Box Leadership,* Paul D. Houston observed that schools have been making incremental progress in an exponential environment, one in which "deteriorating social conditions surrounding families and children have confronted us with all sorts of new challenges." He called for transformative leadership, which can come only by thinking differently about our problems.

Providing educators and educational leaders with such assistance is one overarching purpose of this series.

Our intent in Volume 3, *Sustaining Professional Learning Communities,* is to look beyond inclusiveness and transformation to the perilously difficult task of holding onto—and improving upon— valuable work once it has begun. The literature of education reform is, unfortunately, replete with examples of beneficial changes that failed the test of time. How can we work together to create learning communities that support enduring change?

In Chapter 1, "Communities Committed to Learning": A Case Story of Building Sustainable Success, Nancy Shin Pascal and Alan M. Blankstein of the HOPE Foundation describe the culture of the Newport News, Virginia, schools—"a learning community with both lateral and vertical accountability intended to ensure the success of *all* children." The story of Newport News, they tell us, illustrates the process of creating sustainable success through constancy of purpose. By means of creating a common vision, communicating expectations personally and persistently, engaging all stakeholders, and focusing on instruction, the district realized unprecedented gains in student achievement.

In Chapter 2, Making the Promise a Reality, Shirley M. Hord (Scholar Emerita, Southwest Educational Development Laboratory) and Stephanie A. Hirsh (executive director of the National Staff Development Council) return to the troubling disparity addressed in Volume 1 of this series: the gap between where we want all students to perform and where most are actually performing. How to close that gap? "The surest way," they say, "to help teachers to help all students is to engage all teachers in professional learning communities." Because all change and improvement depends on learning, they maintain, the professional learning community "provides the environment in which principals and teachers set about intentionally learning in order to increase their effectiveness—and, subsequently, increase student results."

"After more than a decade of studying professional communities, I continue to be struck by the variety of ways in which they emerge— and by their fragility," writes Karen Seashore Louis, Rodney Wallace Professor for the Advancement of Teaching and Learning at the University of Minnesota. (That very fragility led to the creation of this volume.) In Chapter 3, Creating and Sustaining Professional Communities, she observes that educators have an urgent sense that schools— and students—need more than benchmarks and tests if they are to succeed. Professional community means more than creating supportive environments, however. Providing the direction that promotes and sustains supportive relationships under conditions of accountability and uncertainty is an exceedingly demanding task.

Maurice J. Elias, a professor in the Department of Psychology at Rutgers University, posits the image of a school system as "a living organism with interrelated parts and functions . . . [that] complement one another and . . . must achieve balance." In Chapter 4, From Model Implementation to Sustainability: A Multisite Study of Pathways to Excellence in Social-Emotional Learning and Related School Programs, he explains that "the introduction of any new program or initiative must be done with consideration of the overall context of that school system, and with attention to how that program will fit with—and balance with—existing realities." Both healthy implementation and healthy sustainability are vitally important to continuity of interventions for children.

James B. Vetter, a colleague of Maurice Elias and the program director of the Open Circle Program at Wellesley College, asks, "What can help schools sustain and deepen their use of social and emotional learning (SEL) programs over time—and what lessons can these insights offer for sustaining *any* school-based program?" In Chapter 5, A Leadership Team Approach to Sustaining Social and Emotional Learning, Vetter reminds us that "even the highest-quality program can be effective only if it reaches the students for whom it is intended—and does not simply wind up as another box or binder stacked on a cluttered shelf." His lesson is this: "In our experience, when schools foster broad-based leadership and engage in an ongoing planning process, the result is to substantially deepen their use of SEL."

In telling the story of Ettaville, New Jersey, Larry Leverett, another Elias colleague (and former superintendent of the Greenwich, CT, Public Schools), in Chapter 6, Pursuit of Sustainability, arrives at a different understanding of the trials and tribulations inherent in the never-ending search for positive changes that endure. "The pursuit of sustainability at the institutional level remains elusive," he admits, but maybe we also need to take into account the changes that took place in the lives of the "mission warriors" of Ettaville—people whose lives and careers were transformed by having been part of a valuable enterprise, and who continue to spread the word to other schools and districts.

"If schools are to be seen as relevant and effective in the twenty-first century," writes Joseph Aguerrebere, president of the National

Board for Professional Teaching Standards, "mechanisms for making decisions about practice, performance, and outcomes will require that practitioners learn to work together (and learn together) in new ways." In Chapter 7, Using National Board for Professional Teaching Standards as a Framework for Learning Communities, he affirms that the National Board can, through its core propositions and standards, provide a way to frame the content for discussion of a learning community, and to better meet the needs of all children.

Collaboration has the power to raise the ceiling higher than individual effort, maintains Deborah L. Wortham, assistant superintendent in the Baltimore City Public Schools. In Chapter 8, Compelled to Create Collaborative Learning Communities, she writes, "Leadership provides the necessary framework within which professional learning communities are created and sustained. The leader must believe that people can learn and grow together, and must be willing to invest whatever allows that magic to take place."

"Professional learning communities will be an educational force to be reckoned with for years to come," predicts Andy Hargreaves, Thomas More Brennan Chair in Education, Lynch School of Education, Boston College. "But let's not celebrate victory prematurely," he warns in Chapter 9, Leading Professional Learning Communities: Moral Choices Amid Murky Realities. In the end, Hargreaves concludes—and his conclusion hearkens back to the beginning of this series—"the strongest professional learning communities in a nation that appears to have abandoned its poorest children are inclusive, empowered, and activist communities that bring professionals, parents, and others together."

This 4-year series began with the urgent need to engage *all* young people in the work of learning—work with the power to shape the course of their lives. Now, after looking in Volume 2 at the power of out-of-the-box thinking in moving us forward on our journey, we are reminded by Andy Hargreaves of the need for educational leaders to be much more than managers or instructional leaders—"to be leaders of their students, their fellow professionals, their wider communities—and indeed of their societies as a whole in collective pursuit of a greater social good as professionals, community workers, and citizens."

Now there's a goal worthy of all the soul-strength you can muster. As before, it is our fervent hope that we have assisted you in this task.

CHAPTER ONE

"COMMUNITIES COMMITTED TO LEARNING"

A Case Story of Building Sustainable Success

NANCY SHIN PASCAL AND
ALAN M. BLANKSTEIN

*If you're too loose, you don't get the focus, but if you're
too focused, you get prescription, and narrowness, and
rebellion. . . . The holy grail of school reform on a large
scale is large-scale ownership.*

—Michael Fullan *(Leading in a Culture of Change,* 2001)

In districts we serve, there is often great disparity between the
ethnic, socioeconomic, and—not surprisingly—academic achievement of students from one school to another. In the case of Newport
News, Virginia, however, the district and school leadership decided
that they would create conditions to sustain all of their students' success. The lessons learned from this 6-year-long journey are pertinent
to all schools and districts.

DISTRICT BACKGROUND AND OVERVIEW

The story of Newport News illustrates the process of how to create sustainable success through constancy of purpose (Blankstein, 2004; Deming, 1986). By means of creating a common vision, communicating expectations personally and persistently, engaging all stakeholders, and focusing on instruction, the district realized unprecedented gains in student achievement.

Newport News was like many other school districts in 2002. It had accomplished leaders and teachers doing their best, seeking to get better, yet struggling to meet new external accountability standards—the Virginia Standards of Learning (SOL). Over the course of 3 years under the leadership of a new superintendent, the division underwent a metamorphosis—a transformation from a division of committed individuals to an interdependent system of communities committed to learning.

The story of Newport News illustrates the process of how to create sustainable success through constancy of purpose.

The 45 schools focused on a simple, clear, and compelling vision: *All* schools would be fully accredited, and *all* schools would make Adequate Yearly Progress (AYP) under the No Child Left Behind regulations. Newport News is now close to achieving this vision.

In 2005, seven of the eight Newport News middle schools became fully accredited (88%), as did 25 of the 26 elementary schools (96%). As of 2006, all five high schools are now fully accredited.

In AYP terms, 24 of 26 elementary schools (92%) and three of five high schools (60%) made AYP. All five high schools made *Newsweek* magazine's list of the top 1,000 schools for the second straight year.

Most important, the entire district is now committed to a process of continual improvement, and has made collective commitments to *all* students' learning—a critical condition for success (Newmann & Wehlage, 1995).

A NEW DIRECTION?

In July 2003 a new superintendent, Marcus Newsome, began his work by looking for the existing strengths and initiatives in the district. Whereas many new superintendents seek to place their personal stamp on their new district, Newsome felt that it was best to find and build on what was already working. Here's how he did that:

1. Building on Strengths

Newsome began by meeting with diverse groups to determine each constituency's perspective on the current state of the school district. His interviews included students, staff members, the PTA, civic and faith-based organizations, elected officials, and other community groups. Among other things, he learned that the district had begun working with the HOPE (Harnessing Optimism and Potential through Education) Foundation to build professional learning communities through attending conferences, using the *Failure Is Not an Option* materials for staff development, and supporting teams as they developed a model of paired schools. The paired-school concept taps the power of "networking" schools (Hargreaves & Fink, 2006) and is explained later in this chapter.

2. Clarifying and Crystallizing the Vision

In a summer retreat with the Newport News school board, Newsome and the board embarked on a mission to see that all Newport News Schools became accredited. Borrowing a line from the movie *Drumline* (2002)—"One band, one sound"—Newsome declared that the school district "must function as one system with one mission." Data-driven research should guide the vision of a team in which each individual makes a commitment to his or her personal and collective growth and development. They established a 6-year plan built around existing research on what works in schools and captured in the phrase "Communities Committed to Learning." Following this meeting, Newsome recalls a man walking up to him and saying quietly, "I'm one of your custodians, and I can't read. Can you help me?" Here was an indication that the message was beginning to penetrate the minds and hearts of every employee. The man not only received the help he desired, but became a shining example for others to follow.

3. Communicating the Vision

In his first general administrative meeting in the fall of 2003, Newsome threw down the gauntlet. "All schools in Newport News will be fully accredited," he announced. This simple, clear, focused vision was one that all could understand, and one whose success could be readily quantified.

To those in the Newport News community, Newsome seemed to be everywhere: He attended staff meetings at each of his 45 schools so he could be present when school improvement plans were discussed. He engaged the support staff, telling the bus drivers, for instance, "You are the first and last people our kids see each school day. You start the relationship, and it carries over from there into the classroom." It was the first time members of the support staff had received such concentrated and positive attention; they gave Newsome a standing ovation during one of his meetings. He made sure that the entire community understood it was *everyone's* job to meet children's needs.

"Communities Committed to Learning" appeared everywhere: on letterhead, in school bulletins, on student information pamphlets, and on all external communications about the division.

4. Building Trust, Relationships, and the Team

Newsome began a 100-day plan with top district leadership to set the path of "team" versus "individual" staff development. He used examples of winning teams and the literature on the components of an effective team. He believed it was not enough for individual schools to make their goals if the district failed to do so as well. He made it clear that responsibility did not end at the schoolhouse door; all staff members needed to take responsibility for the success of the district as a whole. Just as sports teams win or lose as a team and not as individuals, he wanted his staff to think and act like a districtwide team.

Newsome made it clear that responsibility did not end at the schoolhouse door; all staff members needed to take responsibility for the success of the district as a whole.

Before moving forward with his ambitious plans, Newsome felt it essential to form trusting relations that could withstand the pressures of change that were sure to arise as people were asked to alter their practices. His approach included the following:

- Use professional development to build a common language. The HOPE conferences that were initially attended by both district- and building-level leaders were ideal to jump-start the process of creating a districtwide community of learners, but not sufficient for comprehensive implementation. To develop a common language and framework for action at all levels, two such conferences were collaboratively developed to take place in Newport News, and were attended by all district, building, and school board leadership.

- Meet regularly with principals, both individually and collectively. This is described more fully in the following section on developing accountability.
- Meet and speak with all support staff. Newsome's efforts that elicited a standing ovation from members of the support staff were only the beginning of ongoing communication with them. Support staff, students, and teachers all became part of a regular advisory group to the superintendent.
- Give everyone an opportunity for input. In addition to listening to groups like those mentioned previously, with the input of the district's education foundation and its Department of Human Resources, Newsome developed and administered a 69-item electronic survey designed to assess teacher efficacy and teachers' perceptions about their work environment and their ability to affect student learning. Newsome took actions accordingly. After asking how to best communicate with support staff, for example, he began supplementing e-mail correspondence with paper copies at their request.

5. Creating a Pathway to Success

Newsome used a "years to parity" evaluation model developed by Ricki Price-Baugh (2002) to identify gaps in service and to determine how long it would take each subgroup (economically disadvantaged, minority, limited-English speakers, and disabled students) to meet parity with their counterparts given current progress in implementing change efforts. This report provided the baseline for determining strategies and actions in staff retreats. The report was completed in the late spring of 2004 as the result of an independent curriculum management audit and provided additional information to guide long-term work. Providing an externally developed picture of the gaps also created cognitive dissonance for those who had been locked in "cruising" mode.

6. Celebrating Successes

Newsome created and enabled a variety of celebrations at many levels. At the district level, all the schools that made accreditation or AYP were recognized with customized "pinnacle awards" at general administrative meetings, as well as at televised meetings of the school board. At the end of each year, Newsome reported to the board on the state of the school district.

Mini-celebrations dotted the calendar. Newsome started every general administrative staff meeting with what he called "Good News." Good news could be anything from recognition of the Virginia Department of Game and Inland Fisheries for teaching students how to be environmentally friendly; to receiving a Kiwanis award for Educator of the Year; to obtaining a 21st-Century Learning Centers federal grant; to getting a grant from local organizations such as the Chesapeake Bay Foundation, Wal-Mart, or Target.

DEVELOPING ACCOUNTABILITY AND PROVIDING SUPPORT

Expectations were clearly communicated by district leadership, spearheaded by Newsome. Student success rapidly came to be seen as everyone's responsibility. This message was delivered in multiple forums—it was voiced by district-level administrators, classroom teachers, building leaders, bus drivers, and cafeteria workers. The phrase "Communities Committed to Learning" became the omnipresent district mantra.

Clarity of Intent

The concept of "Communities Committed to Learning" was delivered through more than memos or directives. It was delivered in person, repeatedly, and over time. Newsome talked to individual principals at their schools, then spoke to every teacher at every school in their faculty meetings. In every meeting, he emphasized the theme and the priority goals of the district. He made it a point to be present when they talked about their school improvement plans and to review achievement-gap data with them: "You have the second-highest achievement gaps in the district between white and black students in reading. It is a consistent trend. How did you arrive at this result?"

(He memorized and internalized data—no notes, charts, or graphs—to model that such data were important for the teachers and principals to know as well.) The school staff responded: "We have bused students, poor ones. . . ." Newsome's response was clear: "You have no control over that. Now let's talk about what you *do* have control over." When he left, the faculties had deeper levels of discussion based on the positive confrontations Newsome had initiated.

Another addition, the monthly *Superintendent's Spotlight* newsletter, highlighted student accomplishments and the belief that nurturance must go hand-in-hand with accountability. This nurturance was extended to staff as well.

The concept of "Communities Committed to Learning" was delivered through more than memos or directives. It was delivered in person, repeatedly, and over time.

Newsome had multiple advisory groups, including the Newport News Education Association; a group of local clergy; and the nonprofit Newport News Educational Foundation, an advisory and support group of community business leaders. This last group provided advocacy and funds for various projects, including monitoring teacher satisfaction and celebrations such as the "Salute to Success" dinner honoring national achievement scholars.

Structures for Focus and Support

An accountability office at the district level was created and headed by Ashby Kilgore, formerly the principal at Woodside High School, who developed strategic processes to monitor and evaluate the entire district. She assured follow-through on the Phi Delta Kappa report. (All of its 105 recommendations were ultimately enacted.) Newsome redesigned curriculum and staff development to support that effort and established data teams that looked at districtwide achievement.

In monthly meetings, assistant superintendents and executive directors were required to report on progress toward the district's clear vision. The Office of Equity and Accountability, for example, would report on attendance, an AYP measurement. They broke down demographics of data, looking at it in exactly the way AYP would: poverty, disability, and so forth.

New initiatives aimed at the achievement of *all* students required training of all administrators. A new data system, SOLAR (Standards of Learning Assessment Resource), implemented districtwide, allowed principals and teachers to disaggregate data by ethnicity or by AYP measure.

These meetings set the tone for work that had to be done. Reports were generated and reviewed for the population as a whole. A "pyramid of interventions" (Blankstein, 2004) was being developed for each school in the division (see Figure 1.1). Just as schools developed pyramids of interventions for their students (those interventions with the broadest application are at the base of the pyramid, with subsequent levels targeting smaller and smaller groups as you move toward the top), the district developed pyramids of interventions for their schools, analyzing their strengths and weaknesses and providing support at the broadest levels for schools having the most difficulty, and more targeted interventions as schools became more and more successful. Everyone was expected to continue to get better, no matter how well they did.

Elementary principals also had cross-district meetings. At the high school level, in order to graduate in Virginia, students had to

Figure 1.1   Pyramid of Interventions

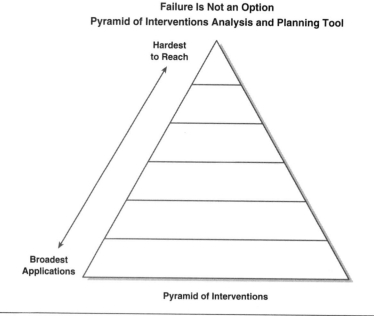

Failure Is Not an Option
Pyramid of Interventions Analysis and Planning Tool

Hardest to Reach

Broadest Applications

Pyramid of Interventions

SOURCE: Reprinted with permission of Alan M. Blankstein and the HOPE Foundation.

earn verified credits on Virginia Standards of Learning tests. At the beginning of each year, high school principals and administrators were charged with identifying those juniors and seniors who were in danger of not graduating. In addition, each school had a pyramid to support every student. Each student had what amounted to an individualized academic plan so he or she would have access to whatever resources were needed in order to graduate.

Newsome requested regular reports that would allow him to track progress. In senior staff meetings, he made it clear that staff members were expected to bring information forward. He always gave deadlines, and staff knew exactly what he wanted to see by that deadline. Minutes from each meeting were logged in chart form, as were tasks to be completed, names of responsible persons, and expected completion dates. Monday morning meetings became the check-in time.

Elementary Pairs

In 2002, the district received a DeWitt Wallace–*Reader's Digest* Grant to pilot a method for building leadership by pairing each successful principal who volunteered with two volunteer principals in lower-performing schools in an informal mentoring relationship. Mary Ann Hutchinson and Ashby Kilgore were two of the principals tapped as mentors. As they talked and listened at the HOPE Institute in Denver in December of that year, they began to believe that this effort *must* include teachers if it was to succeed. Thus, the "principal to principal" concept morphed into the "team to team" initiative that proved to be the beginning of lateral accountability in Newport News.

Both of these successful principals began by building relationships with their volunteer "mentee" principals. The newly paired principals attended another HOPE Institute together—this one in Sedona, Arizona, in the winter of 2003. They established a strong bond during the twisting, winding "pink jeep" ride they took together, which also served as a metaphor for the trials of the change process ahead. That first spring was devoted to getting to know one another both personally and professionally.

The elementary principals went back and began by having breakfast with the leadership teams. At one of the mentee schools, South Morrison Elementary School, the two principals began by asking the staff, "What is it you don't like about your school?" The answer was resounding: "Our school building."

They immediately set about cleaning up the school and making it more inviting. Abandoned cars were moved from in front of the school, and both the interior and exterior were spruced up. "We couldn't get through the culture barrier until we created a place that people could take pride in," said Betsie Clary, the new principal. She set expectations first for the physical plant, then for student success. The new assistant principal, James Battle, made sure expectations about behavior were clear to students, staff, and parents, with consequences for noncompliance that were known by all and consistently enforced.

The two principals asked the staff of South Morrison such challenging questions as, "What would you want this school to be like if your child went here?" They used "Conducting an Educational Garage Sale," an activity from *The Shaping School Culture Fieldbook* (Peterson & Deal, 2002), to determine what aspects of school culture to keep and celebrate and what aspects to transform or change. Items that deserved to be honored because they had served the school well but were no longer relevant went to the "museum." Some were "not for sale," because they were thought to be positive features of the school; at the other end of the spectrum, some highly toxic items that needed to be handled carefully were deposited in the "toxic waste handler."

The two principals asked the staff of South Morrison such challenging questions as, "What would you want this school to be like if your child went here?"

Building Trust

The district helped by staging team-building activities at retreats. In one activity, the staff of South Morrison lined up across from each other and criss-crossed their hands like a train track, bumping the principal down the tracks from one end to the other while their new assistant principal, James Battle, coached the teachers, paraprofessionals, kitchen workers, and custodians in the line.

Clary and Battle reached out to parents by making phone calls and personal visits, and creating an open-door policy. If parents came in, they stopped what they were doing to meet with them.

Formal visits to McIntosh Elementary, the mentor school, were structured as walk-throughs where pairs of teachers would visit classrooms for 15–20 minutes. They observed and talked to teachers and students to understand why their instruction was successful. One McIntosh second-grade classroom employed all kinds of graphic organizers such as thinking maps and Venn diagrams. The teacher was teaching one group, but two other groups of children were working independently at the same time. It was well orchestrated, with children moving and talking, but using "little inside voices." The teacher was using the overhead, so the lights were turned off in that part of the room, but that didn't affect anyone else. Skepticism turned to hope and belief for those who saw this demonstration. "If she can do it," they said later, "so can I."

Some inevitable barriers arose at this point. For example, some resisters came late to meetings or didn't come at all. The leaders were tireless in pursuing their mission to build feelings of trust and team spirit, creating opportunities for conversations at peer-to-peer levels as well as principal-to-teacher. The principals gave teachers a chance to communicate without administrative ears in the conversation. As they began to connect person-to-person relationships, the walls gradually started to come down. Relationships were enhanced when everyone came to realize that the entire change effort was a two-way street: "mentors" could learn from "mentees," as well as the other way around.

Clary's total focus for the first year was on reading. The teams met regularly, committing themselves to Wednesday afternoon for grade-level planning sessions. The two principals collaborated to come up with one or two purposeful questions to focus on in the meetings, such as "What one activity will you use this week for differentiated instruction?" or "What does it mean to work as a team, and how will you show this in your planning this week?"

In the second year, the lead teams started taking the role of shared leadership and making presentations to staff members. That was new and nerve-wracking for staff at first, but has since become quite natural. The ideas were well received because they came collaboratively from peers, not as edicts from administrators.

At South Morrison, the SOL scores continued to go up. Four years ago, this was the second-lowest performing elementary school in the district. Now it is one of the top seven. They made both AYP and accreditation goals.

A MODEL FOR LEARNING *TOGETHER*

At the high school level, the paired school process evolved in a similar fashion. As in the elementary school, the initial focus was all about building relationships. The principals read Michael Fullan's

Leading in a Culture of Change (2001), and decided to focus on reculturing for continuous improvement. They chose three concepts to organize their work: (1) focus on learning and results, (2) professional development for knowledge creation, and (3) collaboration for knowledge sharing.

All participants visited each other's schools. Some teachers visited each other's meetings. The principals worked with the lead teachers. The principals asked such questions as "What is your role as a teacher?" to get some idea sharing going on among the group of lead teachers. There was not much structure to the meetings other than the guiding question.

Initially, those in the mentee schools experienced some resentment, feeling that the mentor schools were coming to tell them what to do. The leaders chose not to bring attention to this resentment, but instead to push ahead. A turning point occurred when the two social studies teams met. The mentee school had better results than did their mentors, and they shared those with the mentor team. This challenged the mind-set of the members of the mentor teachers' group, who modeled a learning disposition: "How can we adopt your approach in our school to get better?" This collaborative approach to learning dissolved the initial defensiveness and helped everyone get beyond the labels of "mentor" and "mentee."

The schools adopted an anthropological model for collective learning. Data gathering about schools was structured like a scientific study, rather than something personal. Both mentor and mentee schools put themselves under the microscope. They developed a form to use across departments. Subgroups picked topics on which to collect data: Structures and Practices, Culture and Symbols, Professional Learning, Leadership, and Results. They attempted to answer the question, "What are the practices and structures in our school that tell kids what our expectations are?"

Groups of teachers developed such guiding questions as "If you had 10 songs in your jukebox, what would they be?" to start the process of documentation. They collected data, and each group set up a display of their findings. Subgroups synthesized the findings and rejoined the whole group to develop a picture of their needs as a school. Each school came to the other and gave feedback on their findings. Warwick High School called it "Warwick's Anthropology: Unearthing Our Practice."

School improvement requires improving the instruction of individual teachers; to get to that, however, it is essential to develop relationships among teachers so they can examine their work in a meaningful way together. Slowly the teams built collective accountability by getting people to begin working together and being analytical together. They did it by deprivatizing practice around an activity that gave teachers permission to ask questions of each other that they would not have had a forum to ask otherwise. The creation of a shared experience meant that all participants had to find the solutions to a common question or challenge *together.* The focus shifted from the exercise being about "me and my classroom" to "it's about the culture of the school." The resulting design focused on examining school culture in order to improve student achievement.

Intervisitations between the mentor and mentee schools became a regular feature of district life. The process involved a premeeting with both groups, in which the host school defines what they want the visiting school to look for, and sets up a schedule of who goes where and when. A response sheet is provided with "look fors" that the visitors check off as they are observed, ending with a debriefing intended to deepen understanding. The visiting school then works on that strategy and has a return visit after several weeks to get more feedback. All of these findings are then presented to a team of administrators and the executive director.

Slowly the teams built collective accountability by getting people to begin working together and being analytical together.

SPREADING LATERAL ACCOUNTABILITY

As a means of developing new leaders and improving instruction, the Newport News district initiated the HOPE Courageous Leadership Academy with 13 volunteer elementary schools. The teams met on Friday afternoons and Saturdays, without extra compensation. As with the paired schools concept, the first year of the academy was spent developing relationships and learning what good collaboration around instruction looks like. The second year focused on normalizing the use of successful instructional strategies across schools, ensuring that they were used broadly and correctly.

"The biggest benefit to me at first was affirmation that we're all in this together," said a member of the South Morrison team, "and the opportunity to really talk to people in other buildings with a structure that focuses your conversations. Informal conversations wouldn't have had as much value, and wouldn't have had the power to help bring about enduring change."

Both peer-to-peer and team-to-team sharing were important. "As we practiced having conversations about larger cultural issues, we were creating building blocks for more targeted and sensitive conversation about instruction," commented Shirley Wilson, a lead team member from South Morrison.

Lateral accountability (Fullan, 2001) was modeled in the academy as school teams reported to one another on the work accomplished in between sessions. The school-based teams, in turn, collectively committed to taking responsibility and being mutually accountable for all students' success in their own buildings. Those teachers who didn't want to live up to the new expectations ended up transferring or being put on a plan of action. Expectations were clear.

People became less possessive of their ideas, wanting to share how they taught and how they organized; they wanted to get better, and they wanted their teammates to get better.

Again, the words of Shirley Wilson, a member of the South Morrison team, speak volumes:

The most important evidence I saw of a culture change was not the walls where examples of the Academy skills were posted. It was in the classrooms: teachers going into each other's rooms and looking and talking—more informal, more collegial, less competitive. People became less possessive of their ideas, wanting to share how they taught and how they organized; they wanted to get better, and they wanted their teammates to get better.

The staff also made a commitment to continuously look at the data. South Morrison now has a K–3 and a Grade 4–5 "data wall." K–1 is based on PALS (Phonological Awareness Literacy Screening) reading scores, 2–3 on PALS and quarterly test scores, and 3–5 on quarterly test scores and SOLs. Individual students have their name recorded on a green index card if they are at or above expectations. Strategic learners (a half to one year below grade level) are on yellow cards; intensive learners (1½ or more years below grade level) are on red cards. The teacher's name is on each card, so accountability is present. All the teachers know that they are accountable for one another and one another's children.

DATA NOTEBOOKS

The use of data notebooks has also become widespread, the development of which clearly signaled the district's commitment to making data-based decisions focused on instruction. These data notebooks are now a part of the fabric of life in Newport News, and are required of every principal and every teacher as a means of tracking each student's progress toward the Virginia Standards of Learning, as well as what interventions or supports will be put in place to ensure that the student meets them.

Each student has an intervention action sheet that teachers develop for him or her, or for their class. At South Morrison, one action sheet might read, "I'm going to teach fractions; here are three things we will do." Principals are required to meet with *all* teachers in the school about their data notebooks. Schools that have not been accredited or achieved AYP meet as a group with their principal and the executive director for their grade level. The conversation centers on "Here's our benchmark data, and here's what we're going to do about it." Principals also have "quarterly data talks" in which the principal and each teacher talk about their data and their plans for intervention. It's important to note that these talks are *conversations,* not evaluations.

LATERAL ACCOUNTABILITY GROWS ACROSS THE DISTRICT

At Warwick High School, the original mentee-paired school, there is a lot of vertical and lateral accountability involving sharing of such data as team minutes and assessment data. Nine-week assessment data on which SOL assessment concepts were missed were tabulated per school, per department, and per classroom, and were regularly reviewed by subject teams and the principal. Each team was accountable to the instructional supervisor, as well as the principal and central office, for creating, implementing, and constantly reevaluating the effectiveness of interventions based on these data.

At the district level, the principals, in concert with their executive directors and the assistant superintendent for instructional services, worked on issues as district problems and implemented them at their schools. The goal was to achieve consistency within and between schools. This practice was fortified by the regular Courageous Leadership Academy meetings at the elementary level, which provide a regular infrastructure for cross-school, districtwide learning and accountability.

Newport News has now initiated districtwide instructional audits. District leadership and school board members are regularly involved in walk-throughs. The audit team includes the coach, a literacy team from another school, and 8 or 10 people from the audited school, in addition to six district representatives or teams from other schools. The district leaders call it "looking at your school through new eyes," and they schedule the audits at least once a month in those schools that need them the most. Conversations before the visits are not about judgments; they are diagnostic, patterned after the medical model. Getting a team that is diverse and includes teachers from other schools as well as teachers from the audited school, along with district representatives, is more important than the details of the process. The important thing is making the work transparent for peers and administrators alike. Those observed will also observe others, gaining perspective and learning to be better diagnosticians, which helps them be better at their own school. Everyone gains by everyone observing, assessing, and learning.

CONCLUSION

Finally, there is the issue of succession planning (Hargreaves & Fink, 2006). Newport News Public Schools has a new acting superintendent, Ashby Kilgore. The board approved her appointment unanimously, and the transition has been smoother than most. The succession plan created upon the departure of Marcus Newsome brought forward leadership nurtured within the district during his tenure. Of the three original paired-school mentor principals, two now serve as district administrators. The third keeps the other two grounded and in touch as she maintains her desire to stay close to the children. Three teachers from the academy and seven teachers from the mentee high school have been promoted to assistant principalships. When Newsome left, the division moved forward without missing a beat.

The Newport News culture—a learning community with both lateral and vertical accountability intended to ensure the success of *all* children—is firmly in place.

This chapter has been a story of constancy of purpose. A vision was created and communicated consistently and persistently, in every venue, supported by actions that spoke louder than words. Leaders at every level were a part of the genesis of the movement; they had a deep understanding of and respect for the vision and the value of the structures and processes that support the vision. The journey is not over, and never will be. But the Newport News school division continues to be a "Community Committed to Learning."

> *The Newport News culture—a learning community with both lateral and vertical accountability intended to ensure the success of* all *children—is firmly in place.*

REFERENCES

Blankstein, A. (2004). *Failure is not an option.* Thousand Oaks, CA: Corwin Press.

Deming, W. E. (1986). *Out of the crisis.* Cambridge: Massachusetts Institute of Technology, Center for Advanced Engineering Study.

Fullan, M. (2001). *Leading in a culture of change.* San Francisco: Jossey-Bass.

Hargreaves, A., & Fink, D. (2006). *Sustainable leadership.* San Francisco: Jossey-Bass.

Newmann, F. M., & Wehlage, G. G. (1995). *Successful school restructuring: A report to the public and educators by the Center on Organization and Restructuring of Schools.* Washington, DC: American Federation of Teachers. (ERIC Document Reproduction Service No. ED387925)

Peterson, K. D., & Deal, T. (2002). *The shaping school culture fieldbook.* San Francisco: Jossey-Bass.

Price-Baugh, R. (2002, May). *Finding 4.1 (Assessment and years to parity): A curriculum management audit of the Anchorage, Alaska, School District* (F. English, Senior Lead Auditor; pp. 159–189). Phi Delta Kappa International. Available online at http://www.asdk12.org/depts/cei/audit/

CHAPTER TWO

MAKING THE
PROMISE A REALITY

SHIRLEY M. HORD AND
STEPHANIE A. HIRSH

As a nation, we say that we want all children to be able to perform at high levels. And yet a gap exists between the level at
which we want all students to perform and the level at which most
are performing. Many people would agree that teachers come to
school, every day, applying all they know to the challenges they
encounter. And yet the gap grows wider. We try to close the gap with
quick-fix programs, with technology, with new tutoring requirements.
Still the gap remains.

What will it take, finally, to close this unacceptable gap? The
answer is this: We as a nation must finally get serious about ensuring that all teachers receive support and have the opportunity to
develop the knowledge and skills necessary to help *all* children succeed in *all* our schools. The gap exists because not all teachers have
the opportunity to develop the skills they need. If these professionals are to become as effective as our children deserve for them to be,
their knowledge and skills must be enhanced, their instructional
strategies must become more powerful, and their application of
strategies must be more appropriately determined and delivered. The
surest way to help teachers to help all students is to engage all teachers in professional learning communities.

The professional learning community (PLC) offers a powerful response to these expectations for increased knowledge and improved instructional practice. Its power resides in its focus on improving an entire school staff, as opposed to improving selected teachers, so that *all* students—not just *some* students—experience high-quality teaching and ultimately achieve at high levels. However, not all PLCs are equally effective. The most successful ones align their practice with the descriptions of the three words in the term:

- *P = Professional. WHO will participate in the PLC?* The answer includes those staff in the school who have the responsibility and accountability to deliver an effective instructional program to students, ensuring that students achieve high standards of learning. PLCs include the administrators, teachers, and instructional support staff, who are counselors, librarians, school psychologists, and others.
- *L = Learning. WHAT will dominate the work of the PLC?* The needs of the professionals are paramount—the content and activities, the knowledge and skills, that they feel are necessary to support improved instructional practice and to increase their effectiveness. The PLC is structured around adults learning so that they develop, over time, the competencies required to ensure successful student learning.
- *C = Community. HOW is learning structured and organized to support educators in advancing their knowledge and skills?* PLCs require structures and processes to leverage the benefit of adult collegial learning.

Just as the work of students is learning, so too is learning the work of the professional learning community. Knowledge and learning are socially constructed and are most fruitfully produced in a social setting with others. The professional learning community offers a structure that accelerates and supports the professional learning of the adults in the school in a community setting. Thus, a professional learning community offers a significant staff development and school improvement approach that contributes to wholeschool improvement and the school's overall effectiveness.

There appears to be broad endorsement of the PLC as a desirable infrastructure for supporting school improvement (among them, Boyd & Hord, 1994a, 1994b; DuFour, Eaker, & DuFour, 2005; Hall &

Hord, 2006; Hargreaves, 2003; Hargreaves & Fink, 2006; Hord, 2004; Louis, Marks, & Kruse, 1996; McLaughlin & Talbert, 2006; National Association of Elementary School Principals, 2004; National Staff Development Council, 2001). Yet there is considerable variation regarding the delineation of the PLC components, as well as how they operate to contribute to the increase of staff learning and competency that, in turn, results in desired student learning outcomes. Research from the literature in school improvement and reform, and from experts' observations and reports of PLC exemplary practice and success in the field, can inform us as to ways of structuring PLCs that have proved to be most effective.

A professional learning community offers a significant staff development and school improvement approach that contributes to whole-school improvement and the school's overall effectiveness.

We write this chapter with the intention of bringing more clarity and precision, more rigor and discipline, to the work of the PLC so that it successfully raises both staff *and* students to higher levels of performance. This chapter explores the critical elements of the PLC that appear to have a range of definitions in the spoken and written commentary on the topic. The more specific we can become in defining the critical elements of the most effective PLCs, the more helpful we can be with schools that are serious about embracing the PLC approach to learning and improvement. Schools considering whether to adopt such a philosophy might benefit from considering the expectations embedded in these elements. These include the following:

- A definition of the professional learning community
- The professional learning community's purpose and value
- The membership of a professional learning community
- Organization of the membership
- Governance of the membership
- The work of the professional learning community

DEFINING A PROFESSIONAL LEARNING COMMUNITY

If one reflects again on the three words that comprise the term "professional learning community," it seems plausible that they convey the idea of the professionals in a school (or other organization) coming together in a group—that is, in community—in order to learn. Members of a PLC are expected to recognize that their learning will be the key to their students' learning. Members of the PLC are expected to acknowledge their own learning needs in their quest to support their students' success. Their true purpose must be improved staff and student performance—and the PLC specifies "learning in community" as the way to achieve this valued goal.

While there are many other important tasks that teachers and administrators complete when they meet in collaborative work groups, a PLC expects them to join the group with the assumption that the data they examine and the needs they identify will point toward the learning they must undertake in order to successfully address the challenges that face them. *Deliberate and carefully constructed learning for adults will produce better results for students.* Learning is always intentional; it is not simply a by-product of the many important tasks that occur among the group members.

From a review and synthesis of the research literature where the work of the PLC, and its results, correlated with improved student learning (Hord, 2004), five components of the professional learning community were identified. These included the following:

Deliberate and carefully constructed learning for adults will produce better results for students.

1. Shared values and vision by the community, wherein individuals identify their own beliefs and purposes for which the school exists, leading to synthesis and agreed-upon common goals that they are committed to pursue for the benefit of students. Without values shared across the group, there can be no community.

2. Shared and supportive leadership, provided by the positional leaders of the school or organization and accompanied by structures and activities that enable staff members to develop leadership capacity, leads to the increasing professionalism of the staff and their assessment of self-efficacy.

3. Collective learning, identified by the community and specifying what the community must learn and how they will go about learning it, is followed by application of the learning across the school, district, or organizational unit.

4. Supportive conditions, of which two kinds are required. The first is physical or structural, such as time for meeting, space for meeting, and other resources such as materials, information, and consultants so that the community can come together to do its learning and work. A second supportive condition is the human or relational feelings or perspectives that the participants have for each other, including respect and high regard for all members, and harmonious attitudes that support learning together.

5. The fifth dimension is peers supporting peers in their improvement efforts, as when a host teacher invites another teacher to visit and observe him or her in a specified teaching activity, after which the visiting teacher provides feedback to the host teacher. This activity engages individuals in learning while observing others, which benefits the visiting teacher as well as the host teacher. In this way, not only do individuals improve, but the organization also increases in effectiveness through the learning of its members.

In essence, the major goal of the PLC is *staff learning together*, with the staff's learning directed to student needs. The staff learning occurs more deeply and richly in interactions and conversations in which staff members pursue intentional learning, share new knowledge, test ideas, ask questions, gain clarification, debate conclusions, and seek consensus on how to transfer new learning to practice.

PURPOSE AND VALUE OF A
PROFESSIONAL LEARNING COMMUNITY

Again, the consistent guiding purpose of the PLC is student learning success. Its undeviating focus on student learning needs drives the content and design of the staff's learning. This can be seen in Figure 2.1. As the initial step, (1) student learning needs are identified; they dictate goals for student outcomes or results. Subsequently, (2) the knowledge, skills, and capacities that staff members (administrators and teachers) need in order to achieve the goals for students are specified. Backward mapping again, (3) professional development nurtures the capacity of the staff so that they gain the knowledge and skills needed to achieve student success. Finally, (4) the system's resources, policies, leadership, and culture are assessed and accessed to provide a supportive context in which these activities are played out.

Figure 2.1   Linking Professional Learning, Teacher Growth, and Student Achievement

SOURCE: Created by Luis Martinez, Southwest Educational Development Laboratory, Austin, Texas.

Figure 2.1 shows how student learning is linked to, and depends on, staff learning. Staff learning precedes student learning, and its focus derives from the study of both student and staff data that reveal specific needs. Thus the staff engages in intentional and collegial learning aligned with needs and goals determined by data. Schools then benefit from the increased knowledge and skills of all staff and subsequent gains for all students.

Additional benefits accrue from these disciplined practices. When a K–12 staff operates as a PLC, individual teachers experience increased morale and have the support of the faculty for the stimulating work of designing and delivering effective learning activities, especially for challenging students. There is a collective "ownership" and responsibility of all the staff for all the students and their needs. As teaching staff learn new ways of delivering instruction, their pedagogy changes. As a result, students engage in higher intellectual learning tasks and achieve greater academic gains. In addition, there are smaller gaps in the achievement of students from different family backgrounds. Staff members work together to focus energy on the mission and purpose of the school: student learning (Hall & Hord, 2006).

There appears to be an emerging interest in professional learning communities at the university level. Institutions of higher education are giving attention to the twenty-first-century skills and attributes needed by university graduates and are employing the PLC structure as a way to encourage the development of such skills in university classrooms. University administrators are supporting this new instructional approach with professional development for the staff's learning (Gonzalez, Resta, & De Hoyos, 2005). It appears that university teacher-preparation programs are recognizing the value of preparing teachers in how to work in PLCs by simulating the culture and experience they want their students to demand when they seek their first jobs.

Staff learning precedes student learning, and its focus derives from the study of both student and staff data that reveal specific needs. Thus the staff engages in intentional and collegial learning aligned with needs and goals determined by data.

Moreover, state departments of education are giving attention to the development of professional learning communities and their operation in schools as a powerful means for school reform and improvement (for example, contact the departments of education for Georgia, Nevada, and New Jersey).

Many educational entities—K–12 public schools, institutions of higher education, state departments of education—are challenging their constituents to give thoughtful attention to student and staff data, and to focus attention on staff learning that enhances the staff's knowledge and skills directed to student learning, so that the potential for clear gains for students escalates.

MEMBERSHIP OF THE PROFESSIONAL LEARNING COMMUNITY

Many educators refer to the "learning community" members as the teachers and students within a school. Sometimes parents are included. Though there is value in these communities of learners, a *professional learning community* refers to the professionals in the school and those at the district level. These are the individuals who have the explicit responsibility and accountability for the successful learning of students. Thus, the focus of attention is properly on the school staff. This means *all* professional staff —administrators, teachers, counselors, media specialists, and so forth. The PLC membership is defined as all those with a line of accountability associated with classroom instruction. This eliminates the school's support staff (secretarial and custodial personnel), who may have suggestions for improving the school, but who are not trained or knowledgeable about quality instruction and do not have direct responsibility for student instruction.

While there are expanding rings of others who exert influence on classroom instruction (school boards, parents, citizens, state departments of education, federal regulators, etc.), it is the immediate professionals in the classroom and school who shoulder the dominant responsibility for student results. These are the members of the PLC.

ORGANIZATION OF THE MEMBERSHIP

With increasing frequency across the United States, school administrators and teachers are using the term "PLC" to refer to their grade-level meetings or subject-area team meetings. To be sure, highly productive team meetings are an essential component of a PLC. But the heart of the work of the PLC is the power of the entire school coming together to determine its goals or the focus of its learning, as well as the work that may be carried out within instructional teams. In this manner, the PLC can serve to help a school keep on track toward its goals.

Without such coordination at the school level, it is more likely that small, uncoordinated teams will develop their own discrete learning agendas, and the benefit of whole-school focus and collegial learning will be lost—and potential impact on the larger school goals reduced. This is illustrated in Figure 2.2 by Scenario A. Scenario B suggests that the subgroups are moving in tandem but may also have individual group goals and objectives.

Without defining the school's focus and following it, individual teams can fragment school improvement efforts just as teachers engaged in individual teaching and professional development planning efforts have done in the past. A school benefits most when all teachers and administrators are pulling in the same direction and determining common messages and expectations for all students.

It is, of course, much easier to schedule time for three to six teachers on a grade-level team or in an academic department to meet than it is to bring together an entire faculty. However, schools are finding ways to ensure that time is set aside for this purpose. As more and more schools prioritize their interest in professional learning communities, district offices may find they can take a meaningful role in helping these schools with the initial challenge of creating time. For example, in some districts, policies have resulted in all schools

Figure 2.2   Aligning Team Activities With School Goals

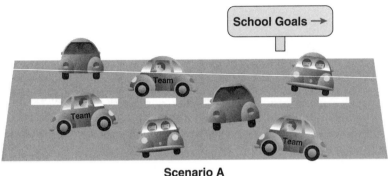

Scenario A

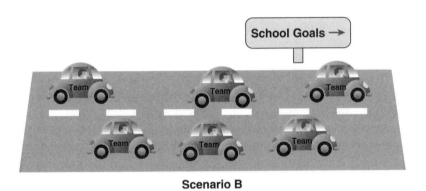

Scenario B

SOURCE: Created by Luis Martinez, Southwest Educational Development Laboratory, Austin, Texas.

dismissing students early one day each week so that the entire school staff can take part in professional learning. There continue to be numbers of schools and systems that create the structures to support these convenings. In some cases, it appears to be more a matter of commitment than available resources. When a school staff comes to recognize that the PLC approach ensures the success of its intentions and efforts, it will find the means to implement all components effectively.

———— ✄ ————

As more and more schools prioritize their interest in professional learning communities, district offices may find they can take a meaningful role in helping these schools with the initial challenge of creating time.

As just one example, there are schools (Boyd & Hord, 1994b) and districts that have extended the instructional day for four days of the week, and shortened the fifth day to create time for staff members to come together. Such rearrangements of the weekly schedule will require the understanding and support of parents, teacher organizations, and other involved constituents. (Some districts have found it possible to engage parents as substitutes to make it possible for teachers to meet. However, many teachers are uncomfortable when students are managed by others than themselves.) Creating a means to dismiss students early or to begin the school day late seems like a workable solution. Schools that have experienced the powerful impact of PLC work have found ways to resolve the time issue (Time for Adult Learning, 1999).

In this chapter, we promote the practice of grade-level and academic teams holding small meetings, and we advocate strongly for the regular and frequent (at least once a month, and twice if at all possible) meetings of the entire staff of teachers and administrators. At this point, let us be clear again in specifying that all the professionals in the building—teachers, administrators, media specialists, counselors—are part of the PLC. The regular convening of the entire staff makes it possible for the school to work together toward learning goals that the entire staff has set and agreed upon.

Imagine an entire faculty convening to examine data, determine student needs, determine teacher learning needs, and create an action plan for addressing those needs. This is the work of the true professional learning community, and the rationale for the large-group meetings of the whole staff. Regular monitoring of the learning and its application is the responsibility of the administrators and leadership team members in order to support the whole staff in staying on track. Engagement in the learning agenda and implementation of the learning strategies are everyone's responsibility. All actions combine to produce the movement necessary to achieve the high expectations we would set for students.

GOVERNANCE OF THE MEMBERSHIP

Any one of us will commit more energy and persistence to issues and projects in which we feel we have a voice. The same is true of teachers and administrators. Democratic participation and the sharing of power and authority are trademarks of community governance and the PLC. The definition of community suggests the development and sharing of leadership responsibilities, including the preparation of school purpose and goals, the identification of learning needs, and the selection of content and strategies for advancing educators' learning and skills. Strong leaders are required for initiating a PLC, but ultimately all members should be supported in developing leadership, and in sharing inclusive leadership across the staff.

The PLC expects that individuals will have voice and choice in their work together, but they will need guidance in how to exercise their new opportunities.

The school staff is more successful at these tasks when it has the opportunity to develop the knowledge and skills to be involved in such actions. Shared decision making depends on the staff's firm base of knowledge and on the skills necessary for engaging in making decisions. Therefore (and this is important), the school staff must develop an array of skills for participating well in a PLC, including the use of appropriate decision-making models to resolve specific questions. The management or resolution of conflict is another necessary area of skill development, as is developing different modes of conversation that can be used for different purposes. Still another requirement for staff members is learning to be active and focused listeners. These skills are best learned at the schoolwide level, and then applied in team settings as well. In addition, schoolwide, staff members benefit from studying and discussing the various stages they can expect to experience as they develop into a high-performing professional learning community.

The PLC expects that individuals will have voice and choice in their work together, but they will need guidance in how to exercise their new opportunities. It is the responsibility of district and school-site leaders to ensure that all PLC members are well prepared to function and contribute in this new setting; otherwise the results will not resemble their goals.

THE WORK OF THE COMMUNITY

Some educators maintain that the major requirement of a PLC is satisfied in those schools that engage staff members in collaborative work; in so doing, they believe, the collaborative work justifies the label of PLC. But if we refer to our earlier definition of a professional learning community, it becomes clear that identified, intentional learning of the staff that leads to student learning is the proper focus of the PLC. *Learning* is its purpose and its function. There are, of course, many ways to engage in learning. Without the clear identification of *what* the staff needs to learn and *how* it will learn it, however, the essence of the PLC is lost.

It is, of course, possible for teachers and administrators to learn when engaged in collaborative work. However, in this case, the learning is the by-product of collaborative work, and may not be what is required to address student needs. Clearly, students will benefit when teacher learning precedes the collaborative work of lesson planning or assessment development (see Figure 2.1). This sequence would appear to produce better outcomes for students. Alternatively, when learning is viewed as the outcome of collaborative work, the students may not benefit until the next time teachers are faced with similar situations and challenges. Ultimately, neither cycle achieves its greatest potential if specific attention is not given to promoting deeper understanding and facilitating reflection. The question becomes this: is the learning what is needed for increasing the effectiveness of the staff? Consider three dessert chefs in an upscale hotel kitchen. Working together, sharing knowledge and skills, they have learned how to produce a very fine banana pudding, of which they are very proud and pleased. But what their clientele really wants from them is crème brûlée! Within this team, there is no expertise that supports the creation of crème brûlée, nor knowledge about where to find the directions. If their learning and productivity is based solely on their collaboration with each other, they will be limited in what they are able to create.

Sharing expertise or repertoires of instructional strategies is another acceptable method that the PLC employs as participants learn with and from each other. However, the learning is restricted to what the PLC members know and the skills that members can share. This strategy is an efficient and effective one as long as the expertise to address a need or goal resides in the group, and as long as careful attention is given to how the others will learn what is necessary to be able to apply the new learning to their classrooms now or in the future.

The PLC should be considered as two dimensions: one is the encompassing shell that provides the structure within which the second part of the PLC takes place—that is, the work of the PLC. The structural shell (the outer circle in Figure 2.3) includes the following components:

- The shared values and vision of the participants that guide their work
- The development of shared and supported leadership that involves everyone in decision making about the work of the PLC
- The structural or physical or logistical conditions that support the operations of the PLC
- The relational conditions—the human attitudes and perspectives, and the regard that the members share with each other
- The peer-to-peer support that members give to each other as they observe each other at work and provide feedback

Figure 2.3   Two Dimensions of Professional Learning Communities

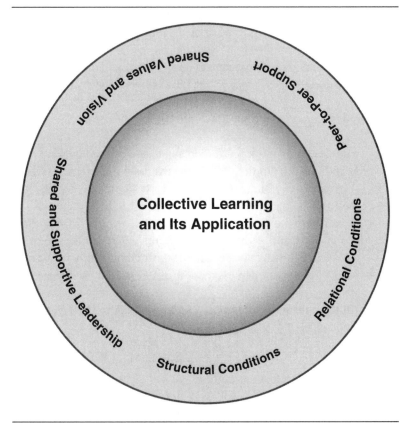

SOURCE: Created by Luis Martinez, Southwest Educational Development Laboratory, Austin, Texas.

These components sustain the work of the professional learning community as it goes about its self-initiated work. Inside this shell, in its heart and soul, the collective learning that contributes unceasingly to quality teaching and student learning—the important work of the PLC—occurs.

It is here that the staff initiates its work through the examination of a wide array of student performance data to assess the productivity of their teaching, and how those data also indicate the students' needs. In most states, there would be expectations that the staff review the data as it reflects student achievement of the state standards. Many school professional staffs do not understand the true meaning of the state standards and their measurement. In addition, there are many schools where the staff members are not skilled in reviewing data, understanding it, and making sense of it for instructional decision making. There is a strong likelihood that there may be a need for *staff learning* in order to develop the skills we have just noted. Thus a vitally important step is checking to determine if the staff needs professional learning for studying and understanding data and applying it meaningfully.

We observe the PLC staff in the details of its work, and note the multiple steps that they employ to conduct their work thoughtfully. (See Figure 2.4 for a simpler description.) It is here that the staff

- *Reflects* on its work for students and related student outcomes as indicated from the data. They evaluate the extent to which their practices and programs are producing the results that they intended.
- *Determines* how well the students are being served (where the staff is succeeding with students' high-quality learning and where it is not so successful) through the study of the data
- *Identifies* student achievement areas in need of attention

Because multiple student needs cannot be addressed simultaneously, the staff also

- *Specifies* priority areas and determines from the data those in need of immediate attention
- *Engages* in studying solutions for the needed areas in order to make decisions about the adoption of new practices or programs. As the staff members broadly explore the most relevant and powerful means for addressing students' needs, they may well require *professional learning* in order to learn about

Figure 2.4   The Work of the Professional Learning Community

- Monitors the plans and implementation progress
- Plans for professional learning and implementation of new practices
- Revises or adjusts based on assessments
- Studies solutions
- Adopts new practices
- Reflects on its work
- Determines how well it is serving students
- Identifies student needs
- Specifies priorities

SOURCE: Created by Luis Martinez, Southwest Educational Development Laboratory, Austin, Texas.

and develop robust criteria for use in selecting new approaches or programs to use in their classrooms. The fact that a school in the next community is using a particular program is not necessarily the best reason for adopting it (Datnow, 1999).

- *Accepts* the need for *staff learning* in order to implement and employ new knowledge and practices effectively
- *Determines* what they will learn and how they will engage in their new professional learning, and *participates* in ongoing learning in order to become proficient with the identified new programs, practices, content, or instructional strategies
- *Plans* collegially for implementing the new learning and then pursues implementation. There is an array of planning templates;

staff would be well advised to *study and learn* about their advantages and disadvantages before determining which to use.

- *Revisits* and *analyzes* the plans and the implementation of the plans with colleagues to assess their success with students. Because this kind of analysis may be new for the staff, *learning* about how to do this may be needed.
- *Revises* or *adjusts* where necessary. With adjustments may come the need for additional *professional learning* about them. With these adjustments and the appearance of new staff learning needs related to student needs, the PLC cycle of improvement continues.

These steps overlap a great deal with each other; some of them are easily integrated with others (see Figure 2.4). The steps of the process may be used with issues and problem solving other than increasing students' academic learning. As one example, we have

Too often, unfortunately, little care is taken to provide staff development that ensures staff members develop deep understanding of content and skills for using new practices.

seen a professional learning community at the high school level use these steps when challenged by the school board to consider the matter of schoolwide uniforms for students. The staff collected and referred to data, focused on specific issues, and did research to expand their knowledge base and understanding of the factors involved in the issue of school uniforms. They undertook an extensive learning agenda to better understand the students' and adults' points of view about the matter and what impact it might have on the school's culture of learning and on students' academic performance. It was a significant learning experience for the staff, and enabled them to make a more authentic and appropriate recommendation to the board.

More often than not, in the typical school improvement process, the staff's learning of new programs and practices is taken for granted. Too often, unfortunately, little care is taken to provide staff development that ensures staff members develop deep understanding of content and skills for using new practices. Such lackluster efforts typically result in the superficial use of new practices and programs. A culture of appearance develops, in which individuals *con*form but don't *re*form—and the results promised by new programs are never realized.

Do not think that PLCs are immune to this distressing and too-common phenomenon. A superficial attention to the work and to the staff's learning would doom any such initiative. As in all change efforts, leaders who act vigorously to maintain the focus have the power to contribute greatly to successful change efforts. Creating and employing the PLC model is most certainly a change for a staff. The likelihood for deeper learning is increased by the thoughtful and consistent attention to the structures and resources that support the PLC, and to the monitoring of the PLC's work by the principal and other leaders—of the small-group teams and the whole school community. There is nothing magical in the PLC structure; rather, its success is determined by the degree to which its members commit to the goal of student learning and embrace their respective roles and responsibilities. That crucial factor is what assures high-quality work. Its effectiveness depends on individuals engaging in the learning and work that the community has determined for itself. When a PLC staff has focused its energies on student benefits, its commitment to the identified student goals encourages staff members in their study and work. This commitment by the whole staff reinforces and motivates the work of the individuals.

Because all change and improvement is dependent on learning, the professional learning community is a structure and way of working that provides the environment in which principals and teachers set about intentionally learning in order to increase their effectiveness— and, subsequently, increase student results. When only *some* staff members engage in individual professional learning, only *some* students will benefit. When *all* staff members engage in PLCs, *all* students benefit. The goal of our schools must be the regular engagement of all educators in professional learning communities

- Where ongoing learning and application of learning is nonnegotiable
- Where goals are established for the entire school, and responsibility is assumed at all levels
- Where acknowledging needs is a sign of strength rather than weakness
- Where teachers recognize that their learning is directly tied to their students' learning
- Where entire faculties have numerous opportunities for celebration of working in the same direction and producing great results for students

REFERENCES

Boyd, V., & Hord, S. M. (1994a). *Principals and the new paradigm: Schools as learning communities.* Paper presented at the annual meeting of the American Educational Research Association, New Orleans.

Boyd, V., & Hord, S. M. (1994b). Schools as learning communities. *Issues . . . About Change, 4*(1).

Datnow, A. (1999). *How schools choose externally developed reform designs* (Report No. 35). Baltimore: Center for Research on the Education of Students Placed at Risk.

DuFour, R., Eaker, R., & DuFour, R. (2005). *On common ground: The power of professional learning communities.* Bloomington, IN: Solution Tree.

Gonzalez, C. E., Resta, P. E., & De Hoyos, M. L. (2005). *Barriers and facilitators on implementation of policy initiatives to transform higher education teaching-learning process.* Paper presented at the annual meeting of the American Educational Research Association, Montreal.

Hall, G. E., & Hord, S. M. (2006). *Implementing change: Patterns, principles, and potholes* (2nd ed.). Boston: Pearson/Allyn & Bacon.

Hargreaves, A. (2003). *Teaching in the knowledge society: Education in the age of insecurity.* New York: Teachers College Press.

Hargreaves, A., & Fink, D. (2006). *Sustainable leadership.* San Francisco: Jossey-Bass.

Hord, S. M. (Ed.). (2004). *Learning together, leading together: Changing schools through professional learning communities.* New York: Teachers College Press.

Louis, K. S., Marks, H. M., & Kruse, S. (1996, Winter). Teachers' professional community in restructuring schools. *American Educational Research Journal, 33*(4), 757–798.

McLaughlin, M. W., & Talbert, J. E. (2006). *Building school-based teacher learning communities: Professional strategies to improve student achievement.* New York: Teachers College Press.

National Association of Elementary School Principals. (2004). *Leading learning communities: NAESP standards for what principals should know and be able to do.* Alexandria, VA: Author.

National Staff Development Council. (2001). *Standards for staff development: Advancing student learning through staff development.* Oxford, OH: Author.

Time: Find it, save it, stretch it, reshape it. (2007, Spring). *JSD, 28*(2).

Time for adult learning. (1999, Spring). *Journal of Staff Development, 20*(2).

CHAPTER THREE

CREATING AND SUSTAINING PROFESSIONAL COMMUNITIES

KAREN SEASHORE LOUIS

I t is safe to say that public scrutiny of educational practices has never been higher. In 1983, when the "rising tide of mediocrity" was identified as a serious issue for U.S. schools, all eyes turned toward the need to increase curriculum rigor. The 1980s saw increasing discussion about the need for "coherence," and both private and public effort went into the design of comprehensive reform models that included attention to professional development, assessment, and student support, in addition to curriculum. At the same time, excessive bureaucracy was blamed for the lack of rapid improvement, and policy makers sought to create more nimble and responsive schools through site-based management and charter legislation. In the 1990s, these trends were joined in most states by an emphasis on clearer expectations about what students should know, and developing better tests to measure whether students (and schools) were doing a good job.

The unremitting concentration on structural and curricular reform has been joined in recent years by a new emphasis on improving the social organization of the school. Buoyed by increasing evidence that leadership and school climate have a significant effect on student achievement (over and above the curriculum and the contributions of individual student characteristics), researchers have begun to pay more attention to how adults work together to create effective learning environments in schools. This "soft" focus on social capacity for change and improvement has been largely ignored by state and national policy makers, who tend to emphasize the use of simpler instruments such as mandates (testing) and system changes (choice, finance reform; Louis, Febey, Gordon, Meath, & Thomas, 2006). Teachers and administrators, however, have been alert to its potential as an instrument to improve their work, and have supported or helped develop many initiatives to increase human capacity, including principal leadership academies, new teacher assessment practices, and improved induction for teachers.

One of the most promising of these initiatives has been the focus on professional communities (PC), or their cousin, professional learning communities (PLCs), largely because they build on the natural strengths of schools and educators (who are generally a cooperative lot), and they require only a rearrangement of existing resources rather than an infusion of lots of new money. In this chapter, I will try to answer several questions about PLCs that are related to its potential as a lever for school reform:

1. What are PLCs, and why would you want one?

2. What are the common mistakes that schools make when they try to initiate and strengthen PLCs?

3. What needs to change in order to have a vital PLC?

4. What are the dilemmas associated with maintaining PLCs?

WHAT ARE PROFESSIONAL LEARNING COMMUNITIES, AND WHY WOULD YOU WANT ONE?

There is substantial agreement about the core characteristics of a professional learning community (Roy & Hord, 2006). First, PLCs involve *collective work* in teams (or the whole staff) in which *leadership and responsibility for student learning is widely shared.* The work of groups of teachers (and administrators) *focuses on reflective inquiry and learning,* with an explicit emphasis on how knowledge *improves student learning.* While there is room for diversity of opinions, there is a core of *shared values and norms* that influence how daily decisions are made in halls and classrooms. Sharing involves the development of *common practices and feedback* on instructional strengths and weaknesses. There is also agreement that in order for these characteristics to persist, schools must address the conditions that support or impede the work of PLCs, including attention to the use of time, the use of rewards, and the development of a positive culture.

The main reason that educational professionals should pay attention is because PLCs have been shown in several well-designed studies to be associated with improved instruction and student learning.

For most teachers, this sounds like heaven on earth. Who wouldn't want to come to work every day in a school that had these characteristics? But schools exist for a larger goal than teacher satisfaction, and the main reason that educational professionals should pay attention is because PLCs have been shown in several well-designed studies to be associated with improved instruction and student learning.

Several years ago, Helen Marks and I looked at the association between professional community, authentic instruction, and student achievement in 24 schools that were selected because they showed evidence of sustained improvement efforts. In these schools, the level of professional community was strongly associated with authentic instruction, which was in turn associated with both standardized student test scores and their performance on written classroom work (Louis & Marks, 1998). A more limited study of the characteristics of PLCs in a large national sample concluded that there was a strong association with younger adolescents' achievement gains (Lee & Smith, 1996). These effects have an impact in both more and less affluent schools: An in-depth examination of 44 classrooms in low-income/high-minority schools suggests that active participation in professional community experiences is associated with student learning (Langer, 2000). Along with colleagues, I am currently conducting a study of how leadership affects learning in 45 typical schools across the United States. The teacher survey data from this study show strong associations between indicators of professional community and the intensity of instruction—particularly the use of instruction that maintains a focus on student engagement in authentic tasks. Among these schools, the presence of shared norms and a sense of collective responsibility have a more significant effect on the use of focused instruction than the individual teachers' race, gender, or experience (Wahlstrom & Louis, under review).

WHAT ARE COMMON IMPLEMENTATION MISTAKES?

Given that a school with strong PLCs is a good place for teachers and students to work, it is surprising that quite a few schools that try to initiate them run into apathy and even failure. While there have been no systematic, large-scale implementation studies, a number of issues that I and others have observed can be suggested.

PLCs as a Program

In a suburban elementary school, teachers worked in grade-level teams on the school's improvement plan, which focused on literacy instruction. They had self-initiated study groups, and were conducting peer observations as part of their work. The busy and well-respected principal, eager to find new resources for her school, attended a workshop in which the work of DuFour and Eaker was discussed. Arriving back at school, she announced that they would be implementing PLCs, and assigned teachers to cross–grade level work groups to analyze the school's literacy data.

What's the problem here? The principal, though well intentioned, failed to assess the existing state of professional community in the school, which was already very high—and increasing. By looking at PLCs as a new program to be implemented rather than a set of ideas that could augment current routines, she undermined the hard work and enthusiasm that had gone into collaborative practice. Ongoing relationships were disrupted to make room for the principal's vision of what PLCs should look like, and teachers (who generally liked the principal) saw PLCs as another new project—one of many in this innovative school.

In a typical case, a principal may claim to have created a professional learning community in a single year using the standard methods of planned change: presenting the idea, getting teaches to set goals, taking a subset of enthusiasts to a conference and helping them to sell the idea to their peers, and holding teachers accountable for meeting their goals (DuFour, 2001). While the principal may believe that he or she has created a PLC, we have found that teachers are uniformly skeptical of this approach.

PLCs as an Instrument for Accountability

In a large suburban district, PLCs were mandated in every school. Each newly organized group was told to select one of the district's learning objectives, and to use the available testing data to analyze how to improve student achievement. At the end of each year, the PLCs were expected to report on their progress, paying specific attention to their use of data.

The cry for more data-based decision making is in the air, and linked to the emphasis on improving student test scores. More than a few school leaders see PLCs as a strategy to increase teachers' focus on student achievement data: if PLCs are intended to promote reflection, why not ask teachers to reflect on data? Though logical, this approach—in which teachers are given specific analytical tasks to carry out—emphasizes the knowledge use component of professional communities to the exclusion of the "soft" side of human development. As Hargreaves (2007) recently pointed out,

> Instead of being intelligently informed by evidence in deep and demanding cultures of trusted relationships that press for success, PLCs are turning into add-on teams of thrown together staff who are driven by data in cultures of fear that demand instant results. . . . PLCs are becoming instruments of technocratic surveillance. (p. 183)

Appointing committees to analyze data and focusing on test score improvement as the goal of PLCs shift attention away from the core emphasis on how teachers can improve the connection between their daily instructional practice and student learning. While PLCs may promote data-based decision making, an exclusive emphasis on data analysis can distract teachers from sharing effective practices. Increased use of data may be one result of increases in professional community, but a mandated focus on data analysis and raising test scores conflicts with the core of PLCs, which involve trusting, shared solving of problems of classroom practice.

PLCs as Job Enlargement

Appointing committees to analyze data and focusing on test score improvement as the goal of PLCs shift attention away from the core emphasis on how teachers can improve the connection between their daily instructional practice and student learning.

A high school in an urban center was asked by the district office to consider designing small learning communities in addition to its recent implementation of a block schedule. As part of this effort, a major scheduling and curriculum reorganization was required, including an initiative to put teachers in touch with community partners who help to implement the themes that were chosen to create specialized foci for the new schools-within-a-school (SWS). Teachers were also asked to adapt their curriculum to ensure that core classes reflected the theme of their new SWS, and to take on increased advisory roles. At the same time, there was a clear expectation that the new SWS teacher clusters would also organize reflective PLCs in order to improve instruction.

Teachers in this school were willing but overwhelmed by the new roles that they were expected to play (only a few of which are described earlier), and by the huge demands of implementing so many new ideas simultaneously. Like many high school teachers, this experienced staff was inundated with multiple requirements, including new curriculum, new ways of relating to students, and increasing emphasis on meeting accountability demands for which preservice training had not prepared them. There is no question that teachers' work has changed over the past several decades—becoming increasingly complex even though the job descriptions have hardly changed at all. If PLCs are added to this increased workload, they are likely to be viewed as one more burden rather than as a way of solving pressing classroom issues.

PLCs or Professionalizing Individuals?

A recent case description of two urban secondary schools makes a different point. In the effort to try and counteract professional isolation, the PLC literature has ignored individual needs. Not all of these needs are pretty—people want to be outstanding and have influence, they hope to gain perks for their classroom in the constant battle for scarce resources, and they have professional dreams that do not overlap with the collective will. If no explicit attention is paid to balancing individual and collective professionalization, micro-politics and behind-the-scenes competition may spiral and undermine the spirit of PLCs (Scribner, Hager, & Warn, 2002).

The point of this cautionary story is that school reform needs to balance individual and collective hopes, fears, and needs. Nearly 80 years ago, the father of modern management theory pointed out that on any given day, employees will come to work with a wide range of attitudes and preferences, not all of which are consistent across individuals, and not all of which can be met (Barnard, 1938). Administrators are as overworked as teachers, and it is easy to overlook the need for individual recognition, reward, and feedback in the effort to promote schoolwide success. Creating a balance between paying attention to individual and group needs requires constant adjustment. However, we know that no matter how well-entrenched PLCs become, most daily innovation and improvement in classroom practices (and consequently student learning) will come from individual reflection and adjustments—although the inspiration and "aha" moments may come in group discussion.

ANOTHER APPROACH: SHIFTING THE CULTURE OF THE SCHOOL

The core of the implementation problems outlined earlier is actually quite simple. The idea of professional community was developed as an effort to integrate two previously distinct concepts: professionalism (which is based on specialized knowledge and a focus on serving client needs) and community (which is based on caring, support, and mutual responsibility within a group). In implementation, the focus is too often on increasing professionalism, while ignoring the problem of community.

A number of studies have concluded that creating *structures* that support PLCs—such as time for teams to meet, giving teachers more influence and responsibilities (distributed leadership), and creating more opportunities for feedback on performance—is important to sustaining activities that are core elements of a professionalizing school (Bryk, Camburn, & Louis, 1999; Louis, Marks, & Kruse, 1996).

However, the results of efforts to restructure have often been disappointing and exhausting. On the other hand, these same studies—and many others—conclude that it is shaping school *culture* that has the greatest impact on supporting and sustaining PLCs. Reemphasizing the importance of culture requires that we balance professionalism and community.

PLCs are, in themselves, a shift away from what many have described as a core assumption of teachers' work: a focus on constant and busy adaptations to classroom activities and individual students. Instead, PLCs emphasize sustained collective attention to recurring patterns of student learning, and how individual teachers' behavior affects it. The most obvious cultural shift is away from individualized routine and its concomitant teacher isolation, and toward an emphasis on an evolving consensus about teaching practice. However, there are other underlying changes that must be in place to support a professional community.

> *Reemphasizing the importance of culture requires that we balance professionalism and community.*

It is not hard to find schools that are characterized by significant pockets of naturally occurring professional communities. A more vexing question is how to create it where it is not already in place, or where its manifestations are scattered and weak. School leaders cannot manage a school's culture in the same way that one can ensure that discipline is maintained and students are assigned to the right classes in order to graduate. A simple "to do" list is a sign that the writer has not actually tried to understand, shape, and change the culture of a school. Likewise, culture cannot be permanently altered in a short time frame—one school year. However, several elements of a school's culture that will help to balance professionalism and community are particularly amenable to influence by a principal or other school leader: commitment, trust, promoting organizational learning, and consistent tailoring of the work to the particular school and the people who are in it.

Commitment Begins at the Top

One of the problems with efforts to change the culture of the school through PLCs is that administrators typically want to change everything but their own work. However, as Robert Quinn (1996) points out, creating deep change in an organization requires the leadership to engage in deep personal change. That commitment must be visible to others in the school: If teachers don't believe that their principal or other school leaders are willing to question how they carry out their jobs, why should they be asked to engage in difficult and fundamental questioning of their own practice? The need for principals, in particular, to work backward from teachers' work to their own work, and to engage in serious questions, with teachers, about how the school is organized and for what purposes (and for whose benefits), might easily be seen as false professionalism. Principals need to be part of PLCs of their own. Quinn's 1996 book, *Deep Change,* will go far toward helping the leader understand the level of change that is required of everyone in the school.

Creating and Sustaining Trust

Why does it take so long to initiate a PLC? One answer can be found in the increasingly robust research suggesting that *trust* is an element of organizational culture that is both critical and routinely overlooked—probably because administrators may not really want to face the music. Trust is the basis for "taken-for-granted" aspects of social interaction—a necessary ingredient for cooperative action, and a foundation for social capital (Coleman, 1988; Zucker, 1986)—but the "problem of trust" is evident in educational settings. Many schools have weak levels of relational trust among the adults who work in and with them, even when there are pockets of high relational trust in small groups of like-minded teachers (Goddard, Tschannen-Moran, & Hoy, 2001). Trust is associated with higher levels of performance on varied measures such as student achievement and parent collaboration (Hoy & Tschannen-Moran, 1999). Conversely, low trust is associated with teacher burnout (Friedman, 1991).

While higher or lower levels of trust can characterize a whole school, the well-understood but little-discussed problem of change is that relationships between teachers and administrators are less trusting than those among teachers (Bryk & Schneider, 2002). This means, of course, that teachers are likely to look cynically at an administrator-initiated change. Furthermore, under suboptimal trust conditions, change creates additional tensions and decreases trust because it disrupts the taken-for-granted aspects of institutional functioning or is inconsistent with existing norms. This finding reinforces the need for leaders to build trust in order to sustain effective change (Keedy & Allen, 1998; Mishra, 1996). However, this may be difficult if there is limited institutional trust prior to a change initiative.

In sum, trust is a precondition for developing PLCs, but few schools (and probably fewer school administrators) have confronted the issue of how to improve this component of organizational functioning. Even in the business literature, there are few serious comparative studies about how to build trust, though some valuable suggestions exist. These include emphasizing a covenant between formal leaders and members—the principals and behaviors that they fundamentally agree upon—as well as a contract, and focusing on the building blocks of trust in the process, trust in one's confidence to participate, and trust in the other participants (Caldwell & Kaari, 2005; Sachs, 1994).

Many schools have weak levels of relational trust among the adults who work in and with them, even when there are pockets of high relational trust in small groups of like-minded teachers.

Promoting Organizational Learning

Organizational learning (OL) as a model for cultural change is based on two assumptions: (1) that common meaning is necessary to collective action, and (2) that change cannot occur unless ideas that challenge the status quo are available. In the learning school, adults work together to gather more information about teaching and learning and then discuss, share, and critique new ideas so that all members understand and can use the new information. The learning organization focuses on continuous improvement rather than "reengineering" or "restructuring," but is not necessarily averse to considering more dramatic innovations. There is evidence to show that schools that engage in more active organizational learning also tend to have higher-achieving students (Marks, Louis, & Printy, 2002).

The appeal of the organizational learning framework is, in part, based on the assumption that creating more effective schools does not merely require identifying a list of structural or instructional characteristics and re-jigging the system to implement them. Instead, it is based on a more fluid idea of how change happens. Knowledge, for example, may come from many sources:

- Teachers bring *individually held knowledge* from their prior experiences and training that is often difficult for colleagues to access and use.
- *New knowledge is generated by self-appraisal,* as a result of evaluations, action research, or accountability information. These data can be turned into commonly held knowledge only when there is a shared vocabulary and incentives to discuss "findings." Joint small-group planning periods, regular faculty meetings devoted to discussion, and frequent lateral communication networks provide organizational designs for acquiring information.
- *Knowledge is gained by organized search efforts.* Search efforts vary depending on the energy devoted to them and the absorptive capacity of the organization to take in and use new ideas to create alternative organizational structures and ideas (Louis, 1994). Most concur that the lack of an organized search for high-quality knowledge is a weak point in public education, which has been generously characterized as faddish. It is here that administrators may have the biggest impact, as they carry out the role of intellectual leadership, helping to find and sort information.

Once schools have a clearer understanding of the knowledge resources that they have or must create, they also need *mechanisms for sharing new ideas.* Again, this is an area in which school leaders have enormous influence because they are often responsible for supporting formal and informal opportunities for exchange. Information distribution involves more than placing photocopied articles in teacher mailboxes, and a 10-minute discussion at a staff meeting is no substitute for sustained conversation that can link ideas to action. Instead, organizational learning calls for the construction of meaningful contexts and conditions under which new routines are *demonstrated or practiced* rather than merely discussed.

Information distribution involves more than placing photocopied articles in teacher mailboxes, and a 10-minute discussion at a staff meeting is no substitute for sustained conversation linking ideas to action.

In sum, the ideas underlying an organizational learning perspective focus on continuous change, stimulated by multiple sources of knowledge, where knowledge is a constantly changing collective understanding not of "facts" but of the action implications of what is known together.

Tailoring the Work to the School

Of course, all schools are in a sense similar, but they are populated by students and teachers who bring with them variable talents and preferences, and they are embedded in communities with differing demands and needs. Place matters, and the people in the place matter. While importing new ideas is essential, it is equally crucial to recognize that PLCs in one setting may not operate in the same way in any other setting—even in a school just a few miles away. It is important to keep the guiding principles in mind (those that were outlined at the beginning of this chapter), and to remember that there are many ways to reach the same goal. Some schools might prefer to work in semipermanent teams where trust can be built over a period of time. Others, particularly in small and stable settings, may have high levels of trust and need more stimulation that could arise from multiple overlapping groups and an expectation that new ideas be confronted. It is particularly critical that school leaders recognize what is needed for a school to move forward at any given time, and to coax (not mandate) teacher groups toward active work on that issue.

SUSTAINING PROFESSIONAL LEARNING COMMUNITIES

Andy Hargreaves (2007) recently articulated seven principles for developing sustainable professional learning communities. While I freely borrow from his analysis, my experience suggests a somewhat shorter list of essential tensions that need to be balanced if a nascent PLC is to survive over the long haul.

Depth *and* Breadth

As implied earlier, PLCs (or whatever the school wishes to call its teams or working groups of professionals) need to have the freedom to pursue an important task over a long period of time—whether that is changing literacy instruction or closing the achievement gap in

Elias, M. J., Zins, J. E., Weissberg, R. P., Frey, K. S., Greenberg, M. T., Haynes, N. M., et al. (1997). *Promoting social and emotional learning: Guidelines for educators.* Alexandria, VA: Association for Supervision and Curriculum Development.

Fullan, M. (2005). *Leadership and sustainability.* Thousand Oaks, CA: Corwin Press.

Greenberg, M. T., & Domitrovich, C. E. (2002). *The study of implementation in school-based preventive interventions: Theory, research, and practice.* State College, PA: Prevention Research Center for the Promotion of Human Development, Pennsylvania State University.

Hall, G. E., & Hord, S. M. (2006). *Implementing change: Patterns, principles, and potholes* (2nd ed.). New York: Allyn & Bacon/Pearson Education.

Hargreaves, D., & Fink, D. (2003). Sustaining leadership: Making improvements in education. *Phi Delta Kappan, 84*(9), 693.

Johnson, K., Hays, C., Center, H., & Daley, C. (2004). Building capacity and sustainable preventive innovations: A sustainability planning model. *Evaluation and Program Planning, 27,* 135–149.

Novick, B., Kress, J. S., & Elias, M. J. (2002). *Building learning communities with character: How to integrate academic, social, and emotional learning.* Alexandria, VA: Association for Supervision and Curriculum Development.

Patrikakou, E., & Weissberg, R. P. (2006). School–family partnerships and children's social, emotional, and academic learning. In R. Baron, J. Maree, & M. J. Elias (Eds.), *Educating people to be emotionally intelligent.* Johannesburg, South Africa: Heinemann.

Zins, J. E., Elias, M. J., Greenberg, M. T., & Pruett, M. K. (2000). Increasing implementation success in prevention programs [Special issue]. *Journal of Educational and Psychological Consultation, 11,* 1–2.

Zins, J. E., Weissberg, R. P., Wang, M. C., & Walberg, H. J. (Eds.). (2004). *Building academic success on social and emotional learning: What does the research say?* New York: Teachers College Press.

CHAPTER FIVE

A LEADERSHIP TEAM APPROACH TO SUSTAINING SOCIAL AND EMOTIONAL LEARNING

JAMES B. VETTER

There was a lot of energy around our new social and emotional learning curriculum a few years ago when our school first kicked off the program. All the teachers were trained, and people were excited about teaching skills that could help students get along better and solve more disagreements on their own. But you just don't hear much about the program anymore. Some teachers are still using it, but I'm not sure about the others. How can we make sure this doesn't wind up as another "flavor of the month"?

Things are rolling in our school, but we want something more. We finished initial teacher training and are using the program in all of our classrooms. Now our specialists and other staff are asking how they can get involved. While things are going well in the classroom, we also want to make sure that students use the skills when they need them most, like at recess and in the cafeteria. How can we broaden the program and make it a real school-wide initiative?

E ducators often ask questions such as these as they work to implement a new curriculum or program in their school. What can help schools sustain and deepen their use of social and emotional learning (SEL) programs over time—and what lessons can these insights offer for sustaining *any* school-based program?

In addressing these questions, this chapter draws on the model of the DuBarry Open Circle Sustainability Program, which promotes development of effective school-based SEL leadership teams and helps these teams engage in an ongoing planning cycle to keep SEL program implementation alive and meaningful.

THE OPEN CIRCLE PROGRAM AND SUSTAINABILITY

How to sustain and deepen consistent, high-quality use of a social and emotional learning program has long been a question central to our work at the Open Circle Social Competency Program (www.open-circle.org), a not-for-profit program at the Stone Center of the Wellesley Centers for Women at Wellesley College. Founded in 1987, Open Circle is known nationally as a research-based SEL program with scientific evidence of effectiveness (Collaborative for Academic, Social, and Emotional Learning, 2003; Office of Juvenile Justice and Delinquency Prevention, 2007; U.S. Department of Education Safe Disciplined and Drug-Free Schools Expert Panel, 2001). Open Circle helps elementary schools to support students in developing skills in areas such as communication, impulse control, and social problem solving, as well as fostering positive relationships among students, between students and staff, and among adults within a caring school community (Koteff & Seigle, 2006; Seigle, Lange, & Mackleman, 2006). More than 260 schools in more than 90 urban and suburban communities in New England, New Jersey, and New York currently use the Open Circle Program.

But even the highest-quality program can be effective only if it reaches the students for whom it is intended—and does not simply wind up as another box or binder stacked on a cluttered shelf. The history of school reform efforts has shown that, even with the most widely heralded reform initiatives, often little or no change in day-to-day practice ultimately results (Cohen, 1988; Sarason, 1996; Tyack & Cuban, 1995). On the classroom level (where students actually come into contact with most school-based programs), recommended or mandated "best practices" may be implemented inconsistently, even by teachers who believe they have embraced a new program fully (Cohen, 1990). Many of us who are involved with developing or supporting school-based programs have had the experience of discovering that, following an initial burst of commitment (sometimes including significant expenditures for materials and training), after a year or two—or perhaps only a few months—the favored new program is forgotten, along with other abandoned change efforts.

Achieving effective, sustained implementation is a key issue within the field of SEL. Research on the implementation of prevention programs has shown that without training and support, many teachers who intend to use an evidence-based curriculum never actually use it (Gingiss, Gottlieb, & Brink, 1994), and even trained teachers often discontinue use after the first year (Rohrbach, Graham, & Hansen, 1993). Concerns about inconsistent program implementa-

Even the highest-quality program can be effective only if it reaches the students for whom it is intended—and does not simply wind up as another box or binder stacked on a cluttered shelf.

tion in schools led one group of researchers to worry that, "because young people are not being exposed to the psychosocial-based programs that research has shown to be effective, the public health impact of these strategies has been minimal" (Rohrbach, D'Onofrio, Backer, & Montgomery, 1996). In the past two decades, the focus of SEL program development and research has shifted from simply identifying effective programs and approaches to also supporting schools in sustaining the use of these programs and approaches consistently and effectively over time (Devaney, Utne O'Brien, Resnik, Keister, & Weissberg, 2006).

Since its inception, Open Circle has focused on providing the type of ongoing support that both research (Elias & Kamarinos, 2003) and our own experience have shown increase the likelihood that schools will continue to use a program effectively over time. We offer a detailed, grade-differentiated K–5 curriculum in the context of a program of training and consultation that spans a full school year. Along with 4 full days of training, our core program includes a series of consultant visits to each teacher's classroom to model techniques, observe lessons, and provide opportunities for reflection and feedback. We also provide training in how to use and reinforce Open Circle strategies and approaches for principals and other administrators, for other school staff such as specialists and paraprofessionals, and for parents and other adult caregivers (Open Circle Social Competency Program, 2007).

Since 2001, generous grants from the DuBarry Foundation have enabled us to develop a special Sustainability Program, specifically designed to help schools maintain and deepen use of the Open Circle Social Competency Program. To participate, a majority of a school's teachers must have already received Open Circle training and the school must be able to recruit a leadership team that is available and willing to take part in the Sustainability Program. Participating schools may have a long history of involvement with Open Circle or be newer to the program; of the six schools participating in 2006–2007, two had implemented Open Circle for approximately a decade, while the four remaining schools were in their second or third year of program use.

This chapter will share common patterns of opportunities and challenges teams encounter and other key lessons that may be helpful both for schools that wish to form similar teams to sustain and deepen their own efforts and for program developers, consultants, and others who wish to support schools in this process.

SEL Sustainability: A Team Approach

From both our own experience and the literature on school change (Fullan & Stiegelbauer, 1991; Maeroff, 1993), we have discovered the value of broad-based leadership teams to sustain and deepen SEL work in schools.

Initially, the DuBarry Open Circle Sustainability Program was primarily focused on promoting teacher leadership. Some of the teachers we had trained as consultants to other staff in their buildings had, on their own, developed workshop activities to engage staff and deepen the use of Open Circle and SEL in their schools. We convened a small group of these experienced teachers to refine and document these activities, creating workshops on such topics as building collegial relationships, developing facilitation skills, and integrating SEL with writing and literature.

We have discovered the value of broad-based leadership teams to sustain and deepen SEL work in schools.

The teachers who piloted these designs encountered many challenges, however. They found it difficult to secure time to conduct workshops at their schools and were disappointed by the small number of staff who attended. Many felt burdened by being the lone champions of Open Circle in their buildings and frustrated by changes in the climate in education that made it difficult for their schools to support activities outside of narrowly defined academic areas. While these teachers possessed deep knowledge of their craft, most were not easily able to assess the needs of the wider school community, mobilize broader participation, and navigate the administrative structures vital to getting things accomplished effectively on a schoolwide basis.

From this experience, we revised our model to focus on developing cross-cutting leadership teams whose members represent a wide variety of roles at the school.

Why Build a Broad-Based SEL Leadership Team?

An effective, broad-based leadership team represents the interests and perspectives of a wide range of stakeholders and spreads the workload beyond the usual committed few. We have found that, over time, an effective, comprehensive approach to SEL must extend beyond the vital work of grade-level teachers to include other important members of the school community, such as cafeteria monitors and recess aides; physical education, music, and art teachers; school counselors, psychologists, and social workers; and parents and other adult caregivers. Broadening program leadership to include people from a wide range of these roles can significantly increase the likelihood that the program's reach will extend schoolwide. Developing broader ownership of a school's program can also help ensure that the initiative will survive beyond the tenure of the initial committed champions.

The primary role of an Open Circle sustainability team is to help conduct an ongoing, cyclical process in which members of the school community develop a compelling vision around their use of SEL, assess the current reality of implementation and the context surrounding it, set measurable goals, develop and implement an action plan geared to the school's specific needs and interests, monitor progress, and evaluate results. Throughout the process, the team continues to work to broaden ownership in and commitment to SEL efforts in their school.

Developing broader ownership of a school's program can help ensure that the initiative will survive beyond the tenure of the initial committed champions.

Forming the Leadership Team

Before formal participation in the DuBarry Open Circle Sustainability Program begins, schools must form their initial leadership team, which should typically consist of five to eight members, including the following:

- At least one building administrator (e.g., principal or assistant/ vice principal)
- At least two grade-level classroom teachers who are currently implementing Open Circle (preferably from a variety of grades)
- Other staff members, such as student support staff (i.e., counselors, psychologists, and social workers); special subject teachers (e.g., music, art, physical education); media specialists; and paraprofessionals

Teams may also include other stakeholders, such as afterschool program staff, parents, and system-level administrators. Some teams have explored the possibility of including students from the upper grades in the role of special advisors, if not as fully participating members of the team.

Team members from a range of roles often bring important, complementary strengths. Inclusion of the principal or vice principal can help to ensure administrative support vital to implementation of the team's plans and to a successful schoolwide effort. Involving classroom teachers from a range of grades (especially teachers who are respected by their peers) brings practical, day-to-day experience and increases the team's credibility. Special subject teachers and student support staff may provide key leadership within the team, as their more flexible schedules and their contact with a wide range of students and staff put them in a strong position to support the efforts of the team and carry the work schoolwide. Team members from a variety of other roles can broaden the team's perspective and demonstrate that the effort includes all parts of the school.

In the spring prior to the start of the formal program, we meet with each initial leadership team to lay the groundwork for the planning process. We invite each team to reflect on their school's experience with Open Circle, asking

- What has been the impact of Open Circle on staff and students?
- What are some of the team's future goals for Open Circle at the school?
- How might the team work toward these goals?
- How will they carve out time to do the work?
- How might different team members contribute?
- What results would they hope to see when their initiatives are successful?

We also help teams identify gaps in their initial membership and discuss possible strategies for recruiting others to make the team more representative of the school community. For example, if all teachers on the team are from the lower grades, we might explore how the team can reach out to and engage intermediate-grade teachers. Teams often grow over the course of the year, as their purpose and early successes become visible.

PREPARATION AND INITIAL PLANNING

The overall design of the Sustainability Program is drawn from our model of training and support for teachers who implement our core program. Each teacher new to Open Circle receives a detailed curriculum guide, 4 days of training spread out over the course of the school year, and three classroom visits by a trained Open Circle consultant. Similarly, the DuBarry Open Circle Sustainability Program spans the course of a school year and includes an extensive leader's guide, group training sessions for all teams participating that year, and several onsite consultation sessions at each individual school.

The Sustainability Program begins with a two-and-a-half-day summer institute that fosters team development, offers key concepts and strategies, and provides a framework to support each team in developing a school-specific action plan.

Although part of the same school community, team members may not know each other well or understand each other's perspectives and priorities regarding the school's use of Open Circle and SEL. Institute activities help participants—across teams and within each team—to develop norms for their work together and to share their own personal visions for the future of Open Circle and SEL in their schools.

Principles of Change

To guide their efforts, we invite participants to reflect on what they have learned through their own experiences with school-based initiatives (SEL-related or otherwise)—considering both initiatives that have succeeded and been sustained over time and those that never got off the ground or that arrived with great fanfare only to fizzle or fade away within a few months or years. From their passionate responses, it is clear that many participating educators have had considerable experience with "on paper only" and "here today, gone tomorrow" initiatives. Their experiences typically reflect key principles from overall research on effective implementation of school-based initiatives (Hall & Hord, 2006). These principles include the following.

Change Is a Process, Not an Event

Launching a new initiative (or reviving a fading initiative) requires change, and change takes time. Too many programs are launched without any plans beyond the initial announcement and provision of materials or training. Successful initiatives are reviewed and revised periodically; they include the provision of support over time.

Organizations Don't Change Until Individuals Change

While resources such as materials and funding are important, and structures such as policies and planning documents can help, change really takes place on the level of the individual teachers and other staff who will implement the program over time. Understanding, respecting, and being responsive to the needs and concerns of indi-

Launching a new initiative (or reviving a fading initiative) requires change, and change takes time.

viduals affected is central to the long-term success of the initiative (Evans, 1996).

While Administrator Leadership Is Essential, a Horizontal Approach Is Best

As we discovered while developing the Sustainability Program, the building administrator often plays a vital role in the ongoing success and viability of any program. At the same time, grassroots initiatives by classroom teachers or other staff can also lead to effective efforts. However, top-down efforts can lead to "in name only" initiatives that are forgotten as soon as the classroom door closes. Programs initiated from the top are also likely to disappear when a new mandate or initiative comes along or a new administrator replaces the original leader. Grassroots efforts may be effective in bringing substantial change to individual classrooms or pockets of classrooms (e.g., a particular grade or cluster), but they are not likely to lead to a full, schoolwide initiative. Neither a top-down approach nor a bottom-up initiative tends to be as effective over time as developing broad-based involvement and ownership from a wide range of stakeholders. A more broad-based approach is also consistent with the goal of developing a community of learners (Fullan & Stiegelbauer, 1991; Hall, 1992).

Context Influences the Process

While other schools' experiences can be inspiring and instructive, there is a danger in a school basing its plan too heavily on a standardized model or in measuring success against progress made by other schools. Many factors—such as the specific needs and strengths of the school, available resources, level of support from district administration and the community (or lack of support), basic structures and functions in place (or missing) in the school, and the presence of competing priorities and initiatives—can make an enormous difference in determining useful and realistic goals and benchmarks of success.

The Sustainability Planning Cycle

In the summer institute, we guide teams through a series of steps in an ongoing planning cycle to be used throughout the year and beyond: set a vision, assess current reality, establish goals, create an action plan, check progress, evaluate the results, and adjust the plan (see Figure 5.1). This cycle is modeled on strategic planning processes that have been found to be useful in supporting a range of school-based programs (Center for Substance Abuse Prevention, 2001; National Institute on Out-of-School Time, 2006).

Set a Vision

"If Open Circle was flourishing at your school, what would this look like?" During the institute, team members share individual reflections on this question, then work together to develop an initial team vision. For example,

Our school values the importance of social-emotional learning within the school community. We provide a welcoming environment that embraces diversity within our student population and their families, and we strive to create an accepting, cooperative, and positive school culture by using the principles of Open Circle. The Open Circle Program is an integral, essential, and visible part of our school, and all members of the school community consistently practice its core principles. All members of the community have a vested interest in supporting this school culture.

In addition to helping teams articulate their own vision, we also share our understanding of some of the key elements of broad and deep use of Open Circle, drawn from the experience of schools that have used the program extensively over many years. These elements include nurturing positive relationships; integrating Open Circle concepts and approaches into other areas and activities throughout the school day; providing ongoing training and support

Figure 5.1   The Sustainability Planning Cycle

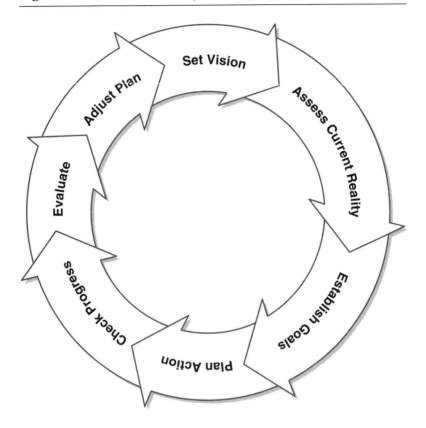

- Determine your vision.
- Assess your overall current reality (strengths, weaknesses, opportunities, threats).
- Establish specific goals and outcomes.
- Map out your strategies and create an action plan.
- Check your progress in implementing your plan.
- Conduct an evaluation and look at your outcomes.
- Adjust your action plan.
- Revisit your vision.

and the cycle continues . . .

SOURCE: Adapted with permission from *Links to Learning* workshop, National Institute on Out-of-School Time at Wellesley Centers for Women (www.niost.org).

for students, staff, parents/caregivers, and other members of the school community; periodically reflecting, assessing, and evaluating; recognizing and celebrating differences and similarities within the school community; and striving to apply SEL skills and concepts in real situations and to act in ways consistent with the principles of the program.

Assess Current Reality

Teams next assess the current situation in their school in comparison with their vision statements and our model of broad and deep implementation. We provide teams with a series of questions to help guide their reflections (see Box 5.1).

Often teams are surprised—and not infrequently dismayed—by what they discover while comparing their current reality with their own vision of a fully embodied, comprehensive approach to Open Circle and SEL. While one might expect this to be true of schools that are struggling, even schools that are proud of their use of the program often discover new avenues they have not explored. All classroom teachers may be trained and on board, but what about the lunchroom aides who may supervise hundreds of children during one of the most socially active times of a student's day?

Teams often uncover questions they are unable to answer. They may know that teachers in the primary grades are using the program faithfully, but what about teachers in Grades 4 and 5? The realization that they cannot answer this question may motivate team members to reach out to intermediate-grade teachers, learn more about their views and experiences, bring these viewpoints into the planning process, and perhaps even recruit some of these teachers to join the team.

A clear understanding of strengths, weaknesses, opportunities, and threats can help teams build on existing assets, anticipate potential challenges, and develop plans that have the greatest chance of success.

As they compare the current reality of Open Circle and SEL in their schools with their ideal vision, teams assess current strengths (e.g., all grade-level teachers are now trained) and weaknesses (e.g., few other staff members are familiar with Open Circle vocabulary and approaches) and consider potential external opportunities (e.g., the new system health coordinator is a strong supporter of SEL) and threats

Box 5.1   Current Reality: Some Questions to Consider

How broad and deep is your school's use of Open Circle and social and emotional learning? Consider the following questions—and make note of questions that your team does not have enough information to answer.

Training and Involvement for All Adults

- How many teachers at each grade level have received Open Circle training?
- How many specialists, administrators, and other staff have received training?
- What has been done to involve parents in Open Circle?

Consistent Implementation of the Open Circle Curriculum

- How often are Open Circle meetings held in each classroom?
- How many core lessons are taught by the end of the year?
- Are the lessons presented fully, including all indicated activities, e.g., role-plays?
- Are the lessons being adapted to meet specific needs of the school, class, or student?

Staff Use of Open Circle Principles and Practices Throughout the Day

- When and how do staff members model use of Open Circle skills and concepts in ways that are visible to students?
- When and how do staff members use Open Circle skills and concepts when students aren't present?

Integration of Open Circle Vocabulary and Skills Throughout the Day

- When and how do staff members coach and cue students to use Open Circle skills at appropriate times outside of Open Circle?
- How are Open Circle skills and concepts integrated into the rest of the academic curriculum?

Schoolwide Activities That Support Open Circle and SEL

• What types of activities make Open Circle visible to the entire population of the school?

Staff Discussions and Reflection on Open Circle Practices

• How frequently is Open Circle included on the agenda at staff meetings (whole staff, grade-level meeting, administration team meetings, etc.)?

Integration of Open Circle With Other School Goals and Initiatives

• To what extent is Open Circle included in overall school goals and integrated into the School Improvement Plan?
• To what extent is Open Circle integrated with other prevention programs?

Adult Community Models of Respect and Caring With Each Other and With Students and Families

• To what extent do staff members treat each other, students, and families in ways that are consistent with Open Circle principles and practices?
• How do adults in the school build community among themselves?

SOURCE: Excerpted from the *DuBarry Open Circle Sustainability Program Leaders Guide*. A full list of Current Reality Assessment Questions is available in the School Leaders area at www.open-circle.org.

(e.g., all energy in the school is focused on sweeping changes to the math and literacy curricula that the superintendent has just mandated). A clear understanding of strengths, weaknesses, opportunities, and threats can help teams build on existing assets, anticipate potential challenges, and develop plans that have the greatest chance of success.

Establish Goals

Once the gap between vision and reality is clear, teams begin to articulate a small number of realistic, measurable goals for the year. Team goals frequently include ones intended to ensure consistent use of Open Circle; to expand training for specialists, paraprofessionals, and parents; to increase visibility of Open Circle throughout the school building; and to integrate Open Circle in broader school plans and activities. For example, to increase program visibility, one school set the goal that visitors would know within 5 minutes of walking through the building that they were at an "Open Circle school"—a school committed to SEL and the Open Circle model.

Create an Action Plan

After setting a few measurable goals for the year, teams begin to map out strategies and create an action plan, with concrete steps they will take to achieve these goals, including who will carry out each task and a timeline for completion.

Teams typically plan activities such as training sessions designed to reenergize teachers whose enthusiasm has started to wane or to include a broader base of staff and parents in the school's SEL activities; formal consultations to support staff in refining and applying SEL-related skills; informal "one-legged interviews"—spontaneous conversations that last about as long as people can stand on one leg and that provide ongoing encouragement and support to staff who are implementing or reinforcing a program (Hall & Hord, 2006); visibility campaigns in which staff or students create posters or other artwork reinforcing program themes or concepts that are displayed throughout the school; and efforts to include discussions of SEL program goals in meetings and to integrate SEL in school planning documents.

Assess, Evaluate, and Adjust

Next, teams decide when and how they will assess implementation and evaluate outcomes in order to determine whether they are on track, identify obstacles, and adjust strategies. Teams articulate questions they plan to ask themselves, such as, "Have the planned training sessions taken place? Did everyone who was expected to participate attend? If not, what can we do?"

They also decide what outcomes they expect to achieve, what indicators will demonstrate progress toward the outcomes, and what methods they will use to gather data related to these indicators. If their goal is to increase consistent use of Open Circle, what results do they anticipate and how will they know this is happening? Will they survey teachers, conduct informal hallway interviews, or review teachers' plan books?

Periodic assessment can also help schools realize when initial goals have been reached and the time has come to establish new goals—and when to revisit and renew the overall vision toward which they are working.

While many educators are very familiar with assessing student outcomes in core academic areas such as literacy, many schools implement SEL programs without much thought of how to assess program outcomes. Although the more rigorous scientific research used to establish programs as evidence-based is beyond most schools' needs and abilities, simpler approaches to assessing key outcomes can provide valuable information to inform ongoing planning (United Way of America, 1996).

Intentionally building periodic assessment into the initial plan can help normalize the type of changes that often need to be made during implementation to consolidate gains and improve strategies that prove to be less than fully successful. Periodic assessment can also help schools realize when initial goals have been reached and the time has come to establish new goals—and when to revisit and renew the overall vision toward which they are working.

The Planning Process Continues . . .

As the teams move through the steps to create an initial action plan at the Summer Institute, we emphasize that what they are creating is a "pre-plan"—an initial sketch to spark their thinking and give them experience with the planning process. Teams are likely to develop an effective plan only by going back to their schools and engaging a wider group of stakeholders. They will also need to repeat the planning cycle every year. Engaging in ongoing planning, action, and assessment can help ensure that potentially effective initiatives are given the necessary time to achieve their promise; that ineffective approaches are discontinued; and that even initially successful approaches are revisited periodically—rather than being institutionalized and continuing indefinitely, whether or not they address current needs. Planning is most effective when it is understood from the beginning to be an ongoing, active process—not a one-time event (Elias, 1997).

While at the Summer Institute, teams decide how they will take this process back to their schools and introduce it to a wide range of other stakeholders. They plan initial concrete steps they can take to achieve early success even as they work to engage others. Teams also determine when they will meet when they are back at school. We have found that teams that schedule regular meeting times (even a brief meeting once a month) are more likely to be successful than teams that say, "We see each other all the time. We'll just catch up and do our planning on the fly."

Before returning to their schools, teams share their pre-plans with other teams to gain perspective and inspiration and an increased sense of accountability.

MOVING FROM VISION TO REALITY

The next element of the year-long Sustainability Program is a meeting with each team at each participating school, typically in October. With the school year in full swing, amid the pressures of many other competing goals and priorities, teams must shift from the energizing "anything is possible" atmosphere of the summer to the day-to-day reality of life in school. Although some teams quickly experience initial success, many find they must adjust strategies and simplify their goals.

Back at school, teams are faced with other staff who are often less committed and enthusiastic than the particularly motivated staff members likely to become initial members of the team. Before adjusting our approach to stress the importance of broadening ownership in the process, we found that after a few months many teams would have a similar complaint:

We came back to our school all fired up with the plans we made this summer. We had lots of great ideas to take Open Circle and SEL to the next level schoolwide—train all of our recess aides, create displays of student artwork on Open Circle themes to hang in the hallways, design a display of books related to Open Circle for our school library, arrange for teachers to observe each other's Open Circle class meetings, and hold a special parent evening about Open Circle. But when we announced all of our wonderful plans to other staff, no one seemed interested! They didn't want to play their part and get involved. What can we do to overcome their resistance and get them to buy in?

We help teams recognize that by engaging others in their planning, they gain a deeper understanding of the needs, interests, and realities experienced by the broader range of individuals who could potentially benefit from the plan—and thus more people are likely to gain a stake in becoming enthusiastically involved. When this happens, more staff members often volunteer to take part in team activities, and team membership grows.

Mid-Year Reflection, Cross-Pollination, and Adjustment

In January, all teams gather for a day-long session of reflection and "cross-pollination," in which they share experiences, strategies, and accomplishments as well as reviewing and adjusting their plans. It is not unusual for teams to arrive with stories of difficulties, unexpected challenges, and distractions, and with some sense of discouragement: "There's so much going on at school. After all our great plans this summer, what have we actually accomplished?" When teams have the opportunity to reflect on what they have done to date, share reflections with others, and receive encouragement and appreciation, they are often surprised to discover the amount they actually have achieved.

Although teams' initial goals often focus on SEL outcomes for students, in the course of their work back at school many teams come to realize that building community and fostering relationships and a positive climate among staff is a key step in the process. As one team member remarked, "We were meeting with staff to plan activities for a visibility campaign around one of our new monthly SEL themes when one teacher said, 'It's hard for us to work with our students on a theme of cooperation when we don't really cooperate all that well ourselves.'"

At the January gathering, we help teams explore ways to help adults in the school community feel connected and capable, believe that they count, and develop the courage to handle what comes their way (Lew & Bettner, 1998). At this point, teams often revise their plans to add goals and activities to increase collegiality and build the adult community within the school. For example, a team organized monthly breakfasts to help staff get

Many teams come to realize that building community and fostering relationships and a positive climate among staff is a key step in the process.

to know one another and feel more connected. Several teams that provided training for recess aides in using Open Circle vocabulary and approaches on the playground found that the aides, in addition to feeling more capable, gained a stronger sense of being a valued part of the staff at the school.

Building positive relationships among the adults in a school can help to create an important, consistent model for students and promote the sense of the school as a learning community. A supportive professional culture in a school can also enhance teacher retention, especially among new teachers who are currently leaving teaching at alarming rates (Murray, 2005).

Sharing Accomplishments

In April, we return to each school for a more extended site visit. This visit provides teams an opportunity to "strut their stuff"—to demonstrate their accomplishments to date. Preparing for the visit may also prompt teams to bring planned activities to fruition, just as people are often more likely to clean and tidy the house before guests visit.

Ongoing contact with Open Circle consultants and with the other teams over the course of the year provides both support and a continuing sense of accountability for the teams' self-established goals—similar to the way that having a coach or check-in partner can help individuals achieve exercise or weight-loss goals.

Celebrating . . . and Beginning Again

In May, all teams gather once more to share accomplishments, review their assessments of progress, reflect on their experiences, and celebrate their successes. We encourage teams to continue developing plans for the following year, reinforcing the idea that sustaining and deepening Open Circle and SEL in their school involves an ongoing cycle of assessment, planning, and action that they can continue in future years.

CONCLUSION

In our experience with the DuBarry Open Circle Sustainability Program, we have been repeatedly struck by the innovative, creative approaches and impressive results schools can achieve by forming an SEL leadership team. Many participating schools have made substantial leaps in broadening their use of the Open Circle Program beyond the classroom by reaching out to include a significantly wider range of staff and parents in their SEL efforts. Schools have increased the visibility of the program—from having posters and displays of student writing and artwork related to Open Circle appear on bulletin boards around the building to conducting special assembly programs and parent events or including Open Circle as part of the regular agenda at grade-level meetings. Teams have often grown in membership, with an increasing number of staff members volunteering to take part, spreading the responsibility beyond one or two initial champions. Climate among students and staff often begins to shift, with teams reporting a growth in positive relationships within the school community. Many participating schools have also reported more consistent classroom use of the Open Circle curriculum and approach as a result of this increased visibility, support, and broadened ownership.

We are currently exploring what types of ongoing assistance may be most helpful to teams after they have completed their initial year of participation in the Sustainability Program. We recently held our first Sustainability "reunion," in which teams from prior years shared ideas and experiences as well as explored their next steps. We are now considering how we might offer elements of the support provided by the Sustainability Program in formats that are less resource intensive, in order to strengthen sustainability efforts in a larger number of the schools currently involved with Open Circle.

In our experience, when schools foster broad-based leadership and engage in an ongoing planning process, the result is to substantially deepen their use of SEL; to develop programming that is targeted to the specific needs and resources of their school; to expand their initiative beyond simple classroom instruction by integrating SEL into many areas of school and parts of the school day; and to carry the principles of SEL into interactions and relationships in the school's adult community. As a result, the schools' use of SEL becomes increasingly relevant and engaging to students and staff alike. And this significantly improves the chance that their efforts will continue and flourish—not simply add another binder or box to a neglected pile on a dusty shelf.

REFERENCES

Center for Substance Abuse Prevention. (2001). *Using CSAP's Prevention DSS* [CD-ROM]. Washington, DC: U.S. Substance Abuse and Mental Health Administration.

Cohen, D. K. (1988). Teaching practice: Plus que ça change. In P. W. Jackson (Ed.), *Contributing to educational change* (pp. 27–84). Berkeley, CA: McCrutcham.

Cohen, D. K. (1990). A revolution in one classroom: The case of Mrs. Oublier. *Educational Evaluation and Policy Analysis, 12*(3), 311–329.

Collaborative for Academic, Social, and Emotional Learning. (2003). *Safe and sound: An educational leader's guide to evidence-based social and emotional learning (SEL) programs*. Chicago: Author.

Devaney, E., Utne O'Brien, M., Resnik, H., Keister, S., & Weissberg, R. P. (2006). *Sustainable schoolwide social and emotional learning (SEL): Implementation guide and toolkit*. Chicago: Collaborative for Academic, Social, and Emotional Learning.

Elias, M. J. (1997). Reinterpreting dissemination of prevention programs as widespread implementation with effectiveness and fidelity. In R. P. Weissberg (Ed.), *Establishing preventive services*. Thousand Oaks, CA: Sage.

Elias, M. J., & Kamarinos, P. (2003, August 8). *Sustainability of school-based preventive, social-emotional programs: A model site study*. Paper presented at the annual meeting of the American Psychological Association, Toronto, Canada.

Evans, R. (1996). *The human side of school change: Reform, resistance, and the real-life problems of innovation*. San Francisco: Jossey-Bass.

Fullan, M., & Stiegelbauer, S. M. (1991). *The new "meaning of educational change"* (2nd ed.). New York: Teachers College Press.

Gingiss, P. L., Gottlieb, N. H., & Brink, S. G. (1994). Increasing teacher receptivity toward use of tobacco prevention education programs. *Journal of Drug Education, 24*(2), 163–176.

Hall, G. E. (1992). Characteristics of change facilitator teams: Keys to implementation success. *Educational Research and Perspectives, 19*(1), 95–110.

Hall, G. E., & Hord, S. M. (2006). *Implementing change: Patterns, principles, and potholes* (2nd ed.). Boston: Pearson/Allyn & Bacon.

Koteff, B. J., & Seigle, P. (2006). Inside Open Circle. In M. J. Elias & H. Arnold (Eds.), *The educator's guide to emotional intelligence and academic achievement: social-emotional learning in the classroom* (pp. 140–149). Thousand Oaks, CA: Corwin Press.

Lew, A., & Bettner, B. L. (1998). *Responsibility in the classroom: A teacher's guide to understanding and motivating students.* Newton, MA: Connexions Press.

Maeroff, G. I. (1993). *Team building for school change: Equipping teachers for new roles.* New York: Teachers College Press.

Murray, J. (2005). *Social-emotional climate and the success of new teachers: A new look at the ongoing challenge of new teacher retention* (Wellesley Centers for Women Report No. 9). Wellesley, MA: Stone Center, Wellesley Centers for Women, Wellesley College.

National Institute on Out-of-School Time. (2006). *Links to Learning workshop.* Wellesley, MA: Wellesley Centers for Women, Wellesley College.

Office of Juvenile Justice and Delinquency Prevention. (2007). *Office of Juvenile Justice and Delinquency Prevention's model programs guide.* Retrieved January 15, 2007, from http://www.dsgonline.com/mpg2.5/TitleV_MPG_Table_Ind_Rec.asp?ID=370.

Open Circle Social Competency Program. (2007). Open Circle Social Competency Program catalog, 2007–2008. Retrieved February 18, 2007, from http://www.open-circle.org.

Rohrbach, L. A., D'Onofrio, C. N., Backer, T. E., & Montgomery, S. B. (1996). Diffusion of school-based substance abuse prevention programs. *American Behavioral Scientist, 39*(7), 919–934.

Rohrbach, L. A., Graham, J. W., & Hansen, W. B. (1993). Diffusion of a school-based substance abuse prevention program: Predictors of program implementation. *Preventive Medicine, 22*(2), 237–260.

Sarason, S. B. (1996). *Revisiting "The culture of the school and the problem of change."* New York: Teachers College Press.

Seigle, P., Lange, L., & Mackleman, G. (2006). *Open Circle curriculum.* Wellesley, MA: Open Circle Program, Wellesley Centers for Women, Wellesley College.

Tyack, D. B., & Cuban, L. (1995). *Tinkering toward utopia: A century of public school reform.* Cambridge, MA: Harvard University Press.

United Way of America. (1996). *Measuring program outcomes: A practical approach.* Alexandria, VA: Author.

U.S. Department of Education Safe Disciplined and Drug-Free Schools Expert Panel. (2001). *Exemplary and Promising Safe, Disciplined, and Drug-Free Schools Programs, 2001.* Washington, DC: Office of Special Education Research and Improvement, Office of Reform Assistance and Dissemination.

CHAPTER SIX

PURSUIT OF SUSTAINABILITY

LARRY LEVERETT

Sustainability of change and innovation in schools and districts is a perplexing problem that has caused me many sleepless nights. The pursuit of sustainability is a core challenge that continues to haunt me and others who have worked with passionate, committed individuals, groups, and organizations interested in doing the right thing for students. We wrestle continually with these questions:

- What is it that makes sustainability so elusive in schools, districts, and communities?
- What are the leverage points that increase the probability that educationally sound innovations can survive the unexpected, unplanned challenges to sustainability?
- Is it possible to achieve sustainability, given the frequent staff and leadership turnover experienced in school districts?

This chapter explores my 7½ years as superintendent in Ettaville (fictional name), a moderate-sized urban school district located in central New Jersey—a school community I deeply appreciate for the significant efforts of several hundred parents, teachers, administrators, school board members, custodians, security guards, and others who worked relentlessly toward a mission in which we all believed, and continue to believe, years later. This chapter will illuminate aspects of the journey of a change-oriented superintendent and the school district/community effort to sustain systemwide instructional improvement with social and emotional learning (SEL) as a major underpinning. I shall also suggest promising strategies for sustaining change and innovation that have the power to survive changes in leadership.

THE CONTEXT

The Ettaville School District took on a bold, low-fat mission statement that became the mantra for the dozens of "mission warriors" who enlisted in the work during a powerful era of hope, promise, and enlightenment. The mission (see Figure 6.1) stirred the passion and commitment of a large, diverse group of people who worked tirelessly to make good things happen for the students for whom we shared the responsibility. This is the mission that I accepted responsibility for, as superintendent, and grew to love. It clearly communicated the belief that *all* of our students are capable of learning and that the responsibility of adults was to do everything we could to help them learn and be successful in school and life. No alibis. No excuses. No exceptions. The mission provided a clear purpose and set a high bar for all concerned with the development of Ettaville students.

Ettaville is a poor, urban school district. Ninety-eight percent of the students are African American or Hispanic. Approximately 70% are eligible for free or reduced-price lunch. When I arrived in 1995, low expectations, low academic performance, a culture of apathy and complacency, and community hostility for failing students presented me with an array of challenges. The district's overall culture and climate

Figure 6.1   Ettaville School District Mission Statement

Ettaville School District Mission Statement

The Ettaville Schools, in partnership with the community, shall do whatever it takes for every student to achieve high academic standards.

No alibis. No excuses. No exceptions.

were largely reactive. Change projects came in bunches and with fanfare, but lasted for short spurts and were inadequately supported. The belief system seemed aligned with the "I've seen them come and I'll see them go" orientation to innovation efforts. An interim superintendent had served for 15 months, prior to my arrival; before that, the board had battled the preceding superintendent for nearly 2 years. The climate was blame oriented and highly fragmented, with little congruence between the work of the central office and that of the schools. Adults seemed more concerned with protecting themselves and less concerned with working across organizational boundaries to advance a student-centered focus.

We pushed back against the existing culture, values, and beliefs that set low limits on what it was possible for students, staff, and community to achieve.

The early work in the district began with efforts to reframe expectations for student performance and to promote the belief (and the confidence) that improvement was necessary and possible. We pushed back against the existing culture, values, and beliefs that set low limits on what it was possible for students, staff, and community to achieve. The era of low expectations for adults and children had to end and be replaced with a vision of high expectations for Ettaville students and adults, based on the ability to succeed in educating all students to achieve in school and in life.

The new district leadership was eager to "fix" everything at once, from instruction and operations to transformation of the culture. During the first year, the administration received community support for a major bond levy and also orchestrated a battle to have the state legislature reinstate the district's eligibility for additional state aid. These resource issues were needed to support instructional goals and ensure adequate funding.

The necessary work in curriculum and instruction for the first 12–18 months was aggressive, but—as we soon learned—quite shallow. The dialogue about the systemic efforts to improve curriculum and instruction was occurring at the district level, but very little of it actually affected schools and classrooms. The dialogue was rich, research based, and anchored in best practice; however, the reality in schools and classrooms mirrored the Hans Christian Andersen story, "The Emperor's New Clothes." We had a good story line, but failed to influence change in practice where it counted. The superficial implementation of ideas and practices had not affected the learning experiences of students in any visible way. Sustainability was not a concern at this point of our work.

Fortunately, a group of critical friends convened and guided us toward focusing on a single systemwide improvement that could be well supported, planned, and executed. We chose literacy as the focus and began the work of identifying best-practice approaches. We committed ourselves to providing our students with a rich set of experiences that required them to think, solve problems, evaluate, and apply literacy skills in powerful ways. We resisted the temptation to rely on workbooks, ditto sheets, and basal readers and embraced the America's Choice balanced literacy framework. A rigorous standards-based approach complemented our interest in helping students learn to use their minds well. The district leadership was intent on doing the "right things" in the right way.

The district challenged the prevailing belief systems that cast doubt on students' ability to engage in a more rigorous program of learning. We quickly learned that this was work that would never end.

Our second major learning occurred at about that same time. The leadership team realized that beyond good curriculum, we had to address the belief systems and efficacy issues of adults and students. The district worked with Jeff Howard and his colleagues from the Efficacy Institute to confront apathy among the students, staff, and community. The work with the Efficacy Institute opened our eyes to the importance of social and emotional skills and competencies in the improvement of academic outcomes. Over a 2-year period, in partnership with the institute, the district challenged the prevailing belief systems that cast doubt on students' ability to engage in a more rigorous program of learning. We quickly learned that this was work that would never end.

Soon after these efforts, we met Maurice Elias, a Rutgers University psychology professor and leading authority on social and emotional learning. Dr. Elias was interested in working with an urban school district to implement a comprehensive program of social and emotional learning. He and his colleagues argued strongly that social and emotional knowledge and skills were the missing components of school reform. We then began to read the literature on evidence-based SEL programs and strategies and learned more about districts and schools that had made a connection between academic achievement and SEL. We committed to having our students engaged in learning experiences that required them to use their minds well and to work hard, and we recognized that the rituals, routines, and expectations of a rigorous standards-based model required the development of SEL. We wanted our students to give and receive feedback, to persevere in the face of hard work, to work collaboratively with others, to have a strong sense of efficacy about themselves and their ability to be successful in school, to solve problems and resolve conflict, and to manage their emotions well.

Hargreaves maintains that "sustainable leadership means planning and preparing for succession—not as an afterthought, but from the first day of a leader's appointment" (Hargreaves & Fink, 2004). We came up short on the first-day criterion, but sustainability was on our minds from the very beginning of this standards-based, systemwide instructional improvement effort. For the next 5 years, our work incorporated the best available thinking on system change and sustainability. Many of these strategies can be found in this chapter. Yet the quality work that involved hundreds of people from across the Ettaville school community, including internal and external advocates and partners, lacked the systemic support necessary to sustain a robust implementation.

This ceaseless pursuit of sustainability haunts me as I explore what we could have done differently, better, or perhaps even not at all, that would have increased the possibility for good results and brought about sustainable effects over time. The literature on sustainability is very helpful for launching and sustaining change and innovation, but is scarce regarding the difficult challenge of sustaining change in the face of leadership succession. This chapter concludes with a few thoughts of a frustrated "nonsustainer" on some approaches that may inform a narrow slice of the problem of sustainability.

THE ETTAVILLE THEORY OF
ACTION TO BUILD AND SUSTAIN SEL

The African proverb, "While the elephants fight, the grass gets trampled," aptly describes the state of the Ettaville district in 1995. The district had many of the characteristics of Terry Deal's definition of a "toxic culture." It was spiritually fractured, focused on the negative, and plagued by misinformation and defensiveness. Hope for revitalizing the school district had long since been devoured by cynicism, negativity, false starts, and a community marginalized by the beliefs and actions of district leadership.

To counteract the toxicity, we needed a clear theory of action, relentlessly communicated and modeled by the superintendent and colleagues at all levels of the organization. The basic components of the Ettaville theory of action included the following:

- Establish a diverse critical mass of staff and stakeholders with a strong commitment to mission.
- Build on this commitment by using pressure and support— pressure to communicate clear and consistently held expectations, and support to help staff to meet the expectations
- Display zero tolerance for alibis, excuses, or exceptions!
- Build community participation and engagement to broaden the base of understanding and commitment beyond the boundaries of the school district.
- Partner with higher education and experts in the field to guide and support the work.
- Maintain fidelity to evidence-based practices and processes to assure consistency across district schools.
- Allocate time and money on a sustained basis to support multi-year implementation.
- Integrate SEL beliefs and principles into all aspects of school district operations.
- Distribute leadership opportunities without regard to appointed or formal position and hierarchy.

The district's theory of action aligned with the recommendations of leaders in the SEL field that identifies the following factors important to sustaining evidence-based social and emotional learning programs in schools. Those factors are the following:

- Presence of a program coordinator or committee to oversee implementation and resolution of day-to-day problems
- Involvement of individuals with high shared morale, good communication, and a sense of ownership
- Ongoing processes of formal and informal training, including the involvement of acknowledged experts
- High inclusiveness of all school populations
- High visibility in the school and the community

- Components that explicitly foster mutual respect and support among students
- Varied and engaging instructional approaches
- Linkage to state goals of schools or districts
- Consistent support from school principals
- Balance of support from both new and seasoned administrators

PORTRAIT OF ETTAVILLE'S SEL IMPLEMENTATION

The following portrait attempts to capture the comprehensive nature of implementation strategies and activities selected to implement the vision of fully integrating social and emotional learning into the culture, norms, values, and beliefs of the Ettaville School District. The portrait is intended to provide the reader with a glimpse of district efforts over 5 school years.

Partnership With Community

Broadening the base of knowledge and exploration of ways to engage the community as a partner in the work of the schools was essential to moving the SEL vision forward. The Board of Education adopted SEL as one of four strategic initiatives for the district, and the administration developed and implemented an operational plan that integrated a range of processes, structures, and activities to include SEL-based beliefs and practices in the school system, as well as specific partnership opportunities with parents and community groups. Internal and external communications were important to promoting engagement and partnership between the schools and the community. We adopted the communications principle that important information must be presented to key audiences at least seven times using seven different ways on at least seven different occasions to reach the diverse information-gathering styles of individuals and groups. The message was consistent and was delivered by a representative cross-section of the Ettaville school community. We were very conscious about the need to "stay on message" to increase knowledge and understanding of the focus and to encourage stakeholders to identify possible roles in advancing the vision.

The oft-repeated message communicated that (1) the mission statement was to be taken seriously and not relegated to a statement that was merely posted in corridors, classrooms, and offices; (2) social and emotional learning was an essential component of the district's strategy to improve student achievement and to influence positive changes in students' social and emotional development; and (3) all interactions with children and their families should be anchored by tenets of social and emotional learning. The district was very conscious about the need to "stay on message" to increase knowledge and understanding of the focus and to encourage stakeholders to identify possible roles in advancing the vision.

Ettaville engaged parents, families, district student support services, community-based organizations, and other partners as participants in learning and modeling principles of SEL. For example, the citywide Parent Teacher Organization (PTO) adopted SEL as its major focus and remained involved in learning to identify their role in support of the district vision, mission, and implementation of the major strategies to get there. Over a period of several years, the PTO led SEL activities that included participation on district committees, SEL presentations at annual parent conferences, advocacy for school and community participation, and participation in parent education workshops. Parents Empowering Parents (PEP), a grassroots group led by parents, organized outreach efforts to other parents and the broader community to advance the SEL initiative. The district supported these efforts with "family liaisons" who worked with PTO and PEP to make the connections between home, school, and community.

Expert Support and External Partnerships

Ettaville would not have been able to sustain the comprehensive SEL initiative without the generous, selfless commitment of Maurice Elias. It was a special day for the Ettaville district and community when Dr. Elias met with the superintendent to explore his interest in implementing a model program in social and emotional learning in an urban district. The wide range of resources he provided included emotional support for the district leadership team; technical assistance and staff development at every point of the journey; brokering resources through his network of researchers and practitioners; the organization of a small army of mission-centered, passionate graduate students; support for assessment projects; advice on structural supports and organizational frameworks; and an endless stream of assistance and encouragement to serve the students and families of

Ettaville. Without his leadership and involvement, this chapter would be a nearly blank page rather than a rich portrait that illustrates the deep change effort that was undertaken with his guidance, support, and caring.

Dr. Elias orchestrated a highly functional team of graduate students to lead a multiyear effort to collect and analyze massive amounts of data from surveys, classroom observations, reviews of pupil performance and discipline data, interviews, teacher surveys, student surveys, professional development participation, and other data sets. The intent was to better understand the impact of our work in schools. The documentation and evaluation effort generated formative assessment data that was used to fuel discussions and decision making on how to organize resources, focus attention, and plan capacity building to address weaknesses in the execution of our approach to systemwide implementation.

The district's efforts were affirmed by a visiting team of SEL leaders from the Collaborative for Academic, Social, and Emotional Learning (CASEL). They observed the following:

Ettaville's efforts to date clearly distinguish it as one of the premier urban leaders in the emerging field of districtwide, SEL-based school reform in the United States. The district stands poised to make a significant contribution not only to the academic, social, and emotional excellence of the young people and adults in Ettaville's schools and community but to the emerging field of SEL-based school reform in general.

Ongoing Staff Development and Resources

Pressure and support were foundation principles in the Ettaville school district theory of action. The district leadership and a critical mass of the Ettaville school community accepted that everyone needed to work differently; the pressure to learn and to apply learning came from a variety of sources, for example, peers, superintendent, parents, principals, and community. High-quality staff development in both literacy and social and emotional learning was valued by many of the staff. The district accepted the responsibility to support staff members with a strong investment in staff development. Participation was not optional; it was expected. Time and money were allocated to support the development of all staff, for example, teachers, school psychologists, guidance counselors, noninstructional support staff, and school- and district-level administrators. Research on effective SEL program implementation and sustainability indicates that well-planned, high-quality professional development, support, and supervision at all levels are essential for success and should have a dedicated funding stream within the school district budget.

The district accepted the responsibility to support staff members with a strong investment in staff development. Participation was not optional; it was expected.

Dr. Elias and his Rutgers University team designed an exemplary series of onsite workshops and targeted technical assistance in the Ettaville schools. The district's adult education supervisor, staff development director, and a district SEL resource teacher designed and implemented annual plans that were modified as specific needs were identified through walk-throughs, and both formal and informal assessments of implementation.

Eventually, the systemwide SEL initiative was established as a line item in the district's annual budget, and a variety of federal and state grant sources were used. SEL spending was further enhanced by the integration of SEL approaches and materials into the budgets in the following areas: Student and Family Support Services, Curriculum and Instruction, Special Services, Early Childhood and Parent Education, and Health Services. The inclusion of SEL supports in these areas was viewed as an indication that progress was being made toward integrating SEL into district operations.

Building a Supportive School and Community Culture

The integration of SEL into the everyday life of the district, schools, and classrooms was at the center of Ettaville's SEL vision. A growing community of advocates advanced the vision-based belief that SEL was an important tool to influence the academic and social-emotional development of Ettaville students. Ettaville used a strategy of "loose" and "tight" methods of guiding schools in the selection of strategies. The district was "tight" on the expectation that schools and departments were expected to either select or develop SEL strategies, and "loose" on the specific activities to be selected. The flexibility was an important means of allowing schools to express their idiosyncratic needs and interests. Being "tight" on a few things assured that all children—regardless of school or classroom—would engage in defined grade-level appropriate SEL programs and activities. As a result, a rich range of classroom initiatives, programs, events, and activities emerged from the school level.

Curriculum and Instruction

Ettaville, like many districts across the country, embraced the standards movement as a means of meeting students' instructional needs. All district schools were engaged in the implementation of a standards-based, whole-school reform model. Given the district's long slide toward low student performance, we felt compelled to keep our eyes on the prize of higher student achievement and thus were careful not to create any diversion from this focus. The district's early reform work targeted language arts literacy, which became a perfect vessel for integration of SEL content. In fact, we found that the SEL skills and competencies were enabling our students to be more engaged in our language arts literacy work.

To achieve success in the balanced-literacy strategies, students needed to manage their emotions, appreciate the perspectives of others, establish positive goals, make responsible decisions, and maintain productive relationships with peers and teachers. Literacy rituals and routines require students to accept more responsibility for managing their own development as learners. Ettaville students were expected to persist through multiple drafts and revisions; to demonstrate the ability to work independently, in pairs, and in small groups; and to accept and give affirming and critical feedback. SEL competencies helped students and teachers focus, persevere, and remain committed to improvement both in relationships and in the core work of literacy. Teachers who were hard-pressed to meet the crunch of curriculum demands recognized the value-added SEL benefits when the amount of time used to resolve conflicts and manage disruptive behavior was reduced because of students having more intrinsic control and greater ownership and responsibility for their academic and social goals. Table 6.1 illustrates the relationship between SEL skills and competencies and the rituals and routines of the standards-based literacy program.

Ettaville curriculum leaders, working with classroom teachers, aligned SEL competencies with the standards established for the selected "New Standards Performance Standards" and the New

Table 6.1   SEL Competencies and Standards-Based Literacy
Rituals and Routines

SEL Competencies	Literacy Rituals and Routines
Self-Awareness	
Identifying emotions Recognizing strengths	Receiving feedback on student work Self-assessment of work products using standards-based rubrics
Social Awareness	

Perspective taking
 	
Appreciating diversity
	Giving feedback, participation in cooperative
	    learning groups
	Collaborative problem solving, multiple
	    approaches to generating solutions

Self-Management	

Managing emotions
 	
Goal setting
	Giving and receiving peer and teacher
	    feedback, using feedback to support
	    revision and correction, accountable talk
	Using standards-based rubrics and feedback
	    to support pacing to meet independent
	    reading expectations

Relationship Skills	

Communication
Building relationships
 	
Negotiations
 	
Refusal
	Author's chair, peer-to-peer editing
	Paired reading, giving and receiving "warm"
	    and "cool" feedback, collaborative writing,
	    data collections and research
	Cooperative learning groups and
	    collaborative problem solving
	Accountable talk

Responsible Decision Making	

Analyzing situations
 	
Personal responsibility
 	
Respecting others
 	
Problem solving
	Integrating feedback using rubrics,
	    conferencing and editing input, portfolio
	    development, reflections, journal entries
	Independent reading, reflections on feedback,
	    pacing revisions to achieve published
	    independent work
	Author's chair, paired/shared reading;
	    peer-to-peer feedback, accountable talk
	Math explorations, collaborative writing
	    tasks, individual and group problem
	    solving, open-ended problems

Jersey Core Curriculum Content Standards (NJCCCS). Alignment was important to fight the "one more thing" fear of principals and teachers that the introduction of SEL would encroach on their ability to focus on the literacy initiative, which was the center of systemwide instructional improvement efforts. We could ill afford any distraction from the student achievement challenges, and alignment and integration were choices that enabled Ettaville educators to address both the academic and social-emotional development of students.

Distributed Leadership

The literature on change, innovation, and sustainability documents the all-too-familiar experiences with short-lived change efforts led by highly capable, charismatic school and district leaders. Another principle of effective SEL programming is the necessity for distributed leadership, broad-based buy-in, and transfer of SEL skills into every aspect of school and community life by administrators, educators, support services staff, parents and families, and community partners (CASEL, 2005).

Person-dependent change strategies were not likely to result in sustained support, and the intent in Ettaville was to implement changes that would be in place over the long term. If sustainability was to happen, it would result from the self-willed initiatives of leaders working at all levels of the school district. Most of us have experienced the adverse impact of frequent turnover of principals, superintendents, and school boards that too often lead to the rapid-fire succession of multiple, poorly supported improvement efforts that are fragile and have short life spans. Ettaville's theory of action relied on many leaders in many different roles who elected to join in sustained demonstrations of collective will and responsibility. The hope was that the good work would survive the departure of leaders and the unintended consequences of shifting priorities. Ettaville deliberately set out to build a "leader-full" organization that would support and model the SEL attitudes, behaviors, and practices aligned with the district SEL vision. District leadership was less concerned with centralizing responsibility, control, and authority within a small group of appointed "officials" and more concerned with providing opportunities for more people to make a contribution that they believed in, were passionate about, and to which they were deeply devoted.

Fortunately, a significant number of people committed themselves to serving as champions and advocates for the full integration of the SEL vision into all aspects of the district culture and operations. Many members of this group led or participated in volunteer roles that encouraged participation, interdepartmental coordination, and shared leadership. The systemic approach to SEL implementation led to new and diverse roles and responsibilities and included the following individuals and organizations: SEL resource teacher, SEL school liaisons, Director of Adult Education, SEL site coordinators, Social Development Coordinating Committee, Social Development Steering Committee, Laws of Life Committee, Student and Family Support Services, Character Education Social Emotional Committee, "T. J. Captains" (a character in an SEL educational video), Rutgers University SEL site consultants, Parents Empowering Parents, and the Board of Education.

Person-dependent change strategies were not likely to result in sustained support, and the intent in Ettaville was to implement changes that would be in place over the long term. If sustainability was to happen, it would result from the self-willed initiatives of leaders working at all levels of the school district.

Monitoring Implementation and Assessing Impact

Ongoing monitoring of program implementation and the use of assessment data served to provide information to a variety of stakeholders that was necessary to build a shared reality concerning the implementation of the SEL initiative. Formative assessment strategies and activities included surveys, interviews, review of report cards and discipline data, and observation of classrooms. All of these served to provide assistance in determining the need for adjustments in strategy or design. Dr. Elias and his band of graduate students significantly expanded the resources available in an area in which the district lacked experience and technical expertise. Fidelity to the implementation of SEL was carefully monitored using a variety of strategies recommended by CASEL (2005).

The district's internal accountability system incorporated expectations concerning the use of evidence-based SEL strategies for students and adults. Information was gathered to determine district and school implementation of a variety of CASEL-recommended strategies intended to increase fidelity to the implementation of evidence-based strategies. The indicators to assess implementation included the number of teacher participants in staff development workshops, the number of teachers using SEL strategies in their classrooms, the level of implementation of strategies in teachers' classrooms, classroom observations using focus walks and walkthroughs, and school- and district-level troubleshooting to identify problem areas.

The assessment of "Talking with T. J.," a video-based SEL curriculum piloted in several third-grade classrooms, studied the changes in students' use of social skills, their acceptance of classroom norms and teacher attributes, their experiences of anger, and perceptions gathered using both teacher and student self-report measures. The study was used to learn what was working well and what aspects of implementation needed adjustment. Results informed decisions about staff development and helped to clarify strengths and deficiencies. For the first time, Ettaville had real data in real time that could be used to increase fidelity and consistency across the involved classrooms. Dr. Elias, with the support of graduate students and a few district staff members, provided follow-up technical assistance with individual schools to engage the participating teachers and principals in review of the data and to tease out implications specific to the school context. The district also used the results to communicate to various stakeholder groups the return on the investment in SEL; these results provided the impetus for expansion of the SEL initiative across the district.

What We "Shoulda, Coulda, Woulda" Done Differently

Reflection is a habit of mind I picked up some years ago as I struggled to identify the meaning and implications of varied experiences during my career in public education. The pursuit of sustainability in Ettaville has been the frequent focus of my musing. I wonder what we could have done better or differently to help sustain the improvement after I left the district. Here are some thoughts:

Board-Superintendent Relationship

Doug Eadie, a consultant to superintendents across the country, appropriately maintains that the board-superintendent working relationship must be close, positive, and enduring—and capable of withstanding inevitable stresses and strains (Houston & Eadie, 2002). Looking back, I accept that my work as superintendent should have included more time and energy invested in the nurturing and development of the school board. I had a laser-like focus on the systemwide improvements, but failed to sufficiently focus on the governing body of the district. I learned my lesson and corrected my practice in my next opportunity to work with a school board.

Board of Education Policy as a Lever for Change

The Ettaville School Board adopted a policy that was intended to institutionalize the responsibility for the superintendent to maintain a districtwide program to meet the social and emotional needs of learners. The policy passed, and so did the requirement to implement the policy stipulations. However, when a board has several hundred policies covering a range of topics—from managing bloodborne pathogens to disciplinary procedures for students carrying firearms—the likelihood that the board will be able to monitor policy implementation effectively is fairly minimal. The policy governance model developed by Dr. John Carver (2006) has great potential as a resource for helping boards to steward their organizations by developing, monitoring, and reviewing their policies. Districts implementing policy governance usually have 50 or fewer policies that they monitor annually. The power of this model is the use of policy as a lever for change and accountability as opposed to the present paradigm of volumes of a policy document that are usually not used or referred to until a problem arises.

Greater investment and support for the personal development of adults was a missed opportunity that could well have yielded benefits to sustainability.

Deeper Integration of SEL Curriculum Content

Ettaville schools would have benefited from the connection of SEL skills with Ettaville's whole-school reform initiatives and the academic curriculum. We also should have made greater efforts to integrate SEL teaching and learning approaches and strategies with district staff development for academic and educational excellence.

More Consistent Modeling by Adults

The adaptation of SEL competencies and skills to adult relationships required more reinforcement. The district incorporated interest-based problem-solving and conflict-resolution strategies to support "getting to yes" on a number of adult issues and concerns, but it never became quite natural for many adults to embrace that the benefits we recognized in SEL for our students could also help us adults in doing our work. Greater investment and support for the personal development of adults was a missed opportunity that could well have yielded benefits to sustainability.

Principal Development

More intense staff development for school principals and other school-based administrators would have added the depth of understanding and commitment needed to support independent behavior that would in turn support sustained implementation of SEL programming. A more effective transfer of leadership from district to schools could have occurred with deeper efforts to position principals and other school-level administrators as sources of intrinsic motivation and SEL implementation. Sustainability is more achievable when principals are motivated, not by a mandate to comply, but rather by a self-determined interest in doing the right thing to create a healthy environment of teaching and learning.

Better Management of Transitions

Too often school districts experience "throw the baby out with the bathwater" transitions that fail to examine what, if anything, should be continued when a transition in leadership takes place. As leaders, we need to do a better job, when possible and where appropriate, of engaging incoming and outgoing leaders in applying the work of William Bridges (1991). Bridges offers some "lessons learned" that may be helpful to all who experience change and transition. He notes that organizations that manage transition well have these things in common. They

- Accept that change and transition are not generally embraced by some
- Establish the context for open, risk-free exploration of ideas
- Focus on interests rather than fixed negotiation postures
- Communicate clear and explicit information about any change and the reasons for the proposed change
- Maintain a commitment to communicate, communicate, and communicate some more

- Involve people in planning and option generation while being clear about decision-making authority for involved individuals and groups
- Keep the mission as the focus

Share Results of Innovation and Make Them Visible

What is success? What's working? Demonstrating the value-added results, using a variety of formative and summative data, serves as an effective demonstration of SEL's positive impact. Communicating across various internal audiences about the benefits helps to build the knowledge and support base important to sustainability. Failure to do so will result in only a few people knowing the benefits, and thereby reducing the opportunity to build grassroots support. Communicate clearly the strong connection between SEL and student performance, school climate, positive behavior, and the relationships between and among students and adults. Sharing successes supports the development of relationships and alliances that spread the good news and increases the possibility of sustainability.

Teachers as SEL Champions

Too often we fail to enlist teachers as resources capable of lending front-line credibility to change efforts. Teachers may not have the position power to promote change and innovation, but they certainly have expert and referent power in their peer-to-peer relationships. They also talk to parents and community members and often have powerful credibility at the grassroots level of the school district or school. Teachers leading and working with colleagues through formal and informal networks can contribute to the credibility of change and innovation in ways that decrees from "above" could not hope to accomplish. Teacher leaders who experience moderate to high levels of success with a particular change or innovation are much more likely to be effective with their colleagues in ways that provide additional legitimacy and support. The investment in developing a large cadre of teacher leaders has great potential for a high rate of return and support for overall goals related to implementation and sustainability.

STANDARDS FOR SUSTAINABILITY

Research for this chapter involved immersion in the literature on managing change, innovation, and sustainability. I was intrigued by Larry Cuban's (n.d.) delineation of a set of standards for sustainability as his contribution to a virtual conference sponsored by the Technical Education Research Center (TERC) that focused on sustainability (TERC Web site: www.sustainability.terc.edu). Cuban's standards recognize the complexity of sustainability and are responsive to the reality of life in schools and districts. The standards should be considered by organizations and leaders interested in sustaining that which is worth sustaining. The standards are presented through the lens of sustaining the implementation of SEL initiatives:

Effectiveness Standard

How did the project perform in meeting the instructional goals? What worked? What were the original goals, and how were they met? Were desired outcomes achieved? What does success mean with relation to such factors as attendance; suspensions; student engagement; discipline referrals; academic performance measures; teacher, student, and parent satisfaction; formative assessment; interview data; and so forth?

Popularity Standard

Everybody likes a winner. "Good news" stories in the media, or recognition programs aligned with SEL vision and goals, are helpful in communicating the benefits for students. Testimonials from teachers, parents, and students who have realized benefits from the SEL investment are also valuable means of communicating successes. The use of symbolic celebrations of accomplishments large and small should occur on a regular basis to reinforce the SEL contributions from all areas of the school district. Success stories that tell of the value-added benefit to students and the teaching and learning environment are powerful means of building a broad base of support.

Fidelity Standard

The assessment of the initial design, with the level of implementation, is a critically important factor. Too often what gets implemented has little resemblance to the initial design. Presence in schools and classrooms—and such protocols as walk-throughs, focus walks, classroom supervision, and observations—are ways to vary the extent to which an implementation gap is present. The absence of information on the fidelity of an implementation places policy makers and administrators at a disadvantage. The adage "inspect what you expect" applies here. If you are not in classrooms and schools monitoring implementation on an ongoing basis, then you probably will not be able to speak authoritatively on the fidelity of the implementation. This means it is necessary to have clear criteria, and thoughtful rubrics, tools, and protocols in place to monitor implementation. The information gathered by these means can provide real-time data that are enormously helpful in making course corrections to improve the quality of implementation. Projects that lack fidelity obviously are not good candidates for sustainability. Large discrepancies between initial design and actual implementation may also suggest that a change strategy may not be a good candidate for being sustained.

Longevity Standard

Cuban correctly observes that many programs never have a chance to stay around long enough to know whether they had the potential to succeed. While longevity alone is not an adequate criterion for making the judgment to sustain SEL, there is something to be said for providing an adequate period of time and sufficient resources before abandoning a change strategy. Longevity, coupled with frequent monitoring and assessment, can accommodate the reality that change is not an event, but rather a process that occurs over time—sometimes as long as 3 to 5 years.

KEEPING HOPE ALIVE

The Ettaville story is a story of triumph and tribulation. Many of the institutionalized components of the comprehensive SEL initiative continue to fade, one by one, as each school year goes by. Sadness and lamentation could be the enduring message about this work.

However, we would thus miss the inside story that is perhaps as powerful as the story of the demise of this noble effort. That story is the change that took place within the "mission warriors" of Ettaville. The people who invested themselves in the work—people who took risks, who engaged in learning and applied those learnings in classrooms, schools, organizations, and perhaps even in their relationships with families and friends.

The story of Ettaville is a story of parents, teachers, administrators, and students who live out their "Laws of Life" in a variety of ways. The internalization of the Ettaville experience by these courageous, passionate, and committed

Sustainability at the institutional level may not have been accomplished in a robust, organizationwide sense, but the value added to the lives and life chances of the hundreds of people involved in this work is being sustained.

people lives on through their continued work. Many of them remain in Ettaville, and numerous others have spread the word to other schools and districts. Sustainability at the institutional level may not have been accomplished in a robust, organizationwide sense, but the value added to the lives and life chances of the hundreds of people involved in this work *is* being sustained. Hope is kept alive through the people who went on from Ettaville to serve as superintendents, curriculum leaders, principals, parent leaders, school board members, college professors, and administrators. They have carried the values and lessons learned along with them to communities far beyond the borders of Ettaville.

The pursuit of sustainability at the institutional level remains elusive, but the redemption just might be that sustainability of the message remains in the good hands and stewardship of countless men and women who have integrated the lessons learned into their personal and professional lives. For this, we are indeed thankful.

REFERENCES

Bridges, W. (1991). *Managing transitions: Making the most of change.* Reading, MA: Addison Wesley.

Carver, J. (2006). *Boards that make a difference: A new design for leadership in nonprofit and public organizations* (3rd ed.). San Francisco: Jossey-Bass.

Collaborative for Academic, Social, and Emotional Learning (CASEL). (2005). *Safe and sound: An educational leader's guide to evidence-based social and emotional learning (SEL) programs* (Illinois version). University of Illinois at Chicago. Available online at http://www.casel .org/projects_products/safeandsound.php.

Cuban, L. (n.d.). *Larry Cuban's reflections.* Technical Education Research Center (TERC). Retrieved from http://sustainability.terc.edu/index .cfm/page/5336.

Hargreaves, A., & Fink, D. (2004, April). The seven principles of sustainable leadership. *Educational Leadership, 61*(7), 9.

Houston, P., & Eadie, D. (2002). *The board-savvy superintendent.* Lanham, MD: AASA/Rowman & Littlefield.

CHAPTER SEVEN

USING NATIONAL BOARD FOR PROFESSIONAL TEACHING STANDARDS AS A FRAMEWORK FOR LEARNING COMMUNITIES

JOSEPH AGUERREBERE

O ur changing world requires different, more effective ways of accomplishing goals. If students are to graduate into a world that expects them to work in collaborative teams, then teachers must model these new ways of working. Learning communities must have a process for working together and content to collaborate about. The core propositions and standards of the National Board for Professional Teaching Standards provide a useful content and process framework for engaging teachers in productive discussions of teaching practice. National Board Certified Teachers, if properly trained, are well positioned to take on instructional leadership roles in learning communities. I'll provide brief examples of two schools that illustrate how National Board Certified Teachers play a critical role in supporting learning communities and bringing about dramatically improved student outcomes. The chapter closes with reflections on issues that must be addressed to ensure success.

A CHANGING WORLD

A vitally important mission of schooling is to prepare students for the world they will encounter and influence. Though the exact nature of the world in which young people will be living is impossible to predict, one characteristic seems inevitable: The world will continue to change rapidly. Technology of the past century narrowed the time and distances that link people and ideas. The twentieth century brought us the automobile and the airplane—surpassing the train and the ship as the preferred method of travel, and moving and connecting people more rapidly than at any time in history. Radio and television provided instantaneous communication and imagery—delivering information and vicarious experiences with the press of a button. At the close of the twentieth century, satellites extended the reach of instant audio and visual communication to anywhere on the globe. The development and widespread use of the World Wide Web and broadband Internet to share information images, both virtual and real, has led us into the twenty-first century with a range of possibilities limited only by human imagination.

A truly global economy is allowing people in all parts of the world to participate, as technology contributes to a leveling of the playing field. The *New York Times* writer Thomas Friedman has observed that a convergence of forces is creating a "flat world," in which the resources to compete are in the hands of the more educated, creative, and innovative (Friedman, 2005).

What does this mean for the world of work? The business community has already figured out that it must work smarter. In concrete terms, this means moving from an assembly-line model for the production of products or services to a team model. This means searching for workers who are skilled and interested in solving problems. Creativity and innovation fuel entrepreneurship, and technology is the new medium for instantly accessing and sharing knowledge. The stimulus for new ideas is more likely to come from environments that support the conditions that lead to creativity and innovation. Peter Senge's work for over 25 years has been devoted to developing learning communities—that is, developing the capacity to collaborate in order to accomplish changes that would be impossible to achieve individually. Individuals with complementary skill sets, when brought together in collaborative groups, are the wellspring of new ideas. A globally competitive environment will assign higher value to those who can create, innovate, and solve problems through networks and collaboration.

IMPLICATIONS FOR SCHOOL ORGANIZATIONS

What does this mean for schools? If schools are tasked with preparing students for a changing world, then educators must be organized to deliver on that responsibility. The current model of teachers as individual performers with a single room of students working in an isolated fashion will not achieve the desired results. Educators must model the new environment in which their students will live and work. Schools built for the Industrial Age are not organized for the new global world. In the past, it did not matter if schools operated as they always have, since the United States led the rest of the world on most education and economic indicators. The trend line has changed dramatically, however, and the United States is no longer at the top on many international comparisons. Given current trends, unless dramatic changes are made, the United States runs the risk of falling further behind and risking an uncertain economic and political future.

Educators must model the new environment in which their students will live and work. Schools built for the Industrial Age are not organized for the new global world.

What must schools do differently to stem this ominous trend? Many steps can be taken to dramatically overhaul how we teach our children so that all students have a real opportunity to participate in the new economy. A key change is in the way that schools and educators organize for teaching and learning. Moving from teaching as an isolated, individual activity to a group orientation is critical.

There are many reasons for providing a more supportive environment for teaching. First, teachers are expected to have a greater command of content knowledge in subject areas that continue to expand with bewildering rapidity. With the tremendous expansion of subject-area knowledge, no teacher can know and do it all alone. They must be supported in developing their content knowledge. Second, the growing diversity of the student population in schools across the United States means that more students come to school with different backgrounds and levels of preparedness. More than at any time in history, students with different language and cultural backgrounds and special needs require teachers to have a wide range of developmentally appropriate pedagogical skills. Teachers need different forms of support to meet the needs of all students. When educators come together in partnership with other educators and work with parents and community resources, the odds for success are greatly enhanced.

A third reason for encouraging teachers to work together is to improve their practice. Teaching should be seen as a profession characterized by clinical practice. That is, knowledge and skills are improved through the actual interaction of students and teachers in a structured clinical setting. If organized properly, teachers with proper training can learn from and help each other. No teacher emerging from a teacher preparation program ever knows all there is to know. Therefore, a structured group in support of improved practice based in school settings can be extremely valuable.

These reasons should not be seen as unique to the teaching profession. It is generally understood that neither a medical doctor, nor an accountant, nor an engineer can rely solely on a university-based preparation program as sufficient training for an entire career. Certainly new breakthroughs and changing societal needs require that practitioners maintain and update their knowledge and skills to serve the public good.

How do teachers develop their practice and get better at teaching? Is there a process in place that allows and encourages teachers to grow? Normally teachers can gain knowledge through acquiring advanced degrees and professional training. Many states require some form of continuing education credits to maintain a license; however, the responsibility rests with the individual. The teacher salary schedule provides additional compensation in return for additional credits and years of experience. Districts and schools may provide professional development opportunities, or mandate particular forms of training, such as how to implement a new curricular program. The effectiveness of this approach has been mixed, to say the least.

The idea that practitioners can learn from each other sounds logical. Then why don't teachers learn more from their fellow teachers?

There are many reasons. First, teaching is seen as an individual, private act. A teacher is assigned a group of students to teach and is responsible for their learning. What actually occurs behind closed doors is usually known only to the teacher and the students. The typical teacher becomes uncomfortable when an adult enters the classroom to observe. When classroom observations do occur, they are usually for the purposes of conducting a formal evaluation of performance. Beyond evaluation and professional development programs, teachers are on their own to determine how to improve. As long as they are

Few practitioners are eager to search out shortcomings, and the practitioner has no structured process in place for engaging in such self-examination.

judged as meeting a passable standard, there is no compelling reason to search out ways to improve. As is true in many professions, few practitioners are eager to search out shortcomings, and the practitioner has no structured process in place for engaging in such self-examination.

Though this state of affairs is not unique to the teaching profession, it *is* a strong deterrent to group learning. Assuming the idea of group learning among colleagues is not established, one must first understand the current environment and be sensitive to the mind-set and social culture of teachers.

An assessment of the current school conditions and history of the faculty must be done before assuming that a school can form professional learning communities and be successful. The assessment should learn as much as possible about the backgrounds of the teachers. It should ascertain the experiences of the teachers, their attitudes toward learning, their years of experience, the achievement levels of their students, existing organizational structures, and group dynamics that may promote or inhibit group learning.

SETTING THE STAGE FOR LEARNING COMMUNITIES

How does one embark on creating learning communities? There is no single answer, but a prerequisite condition is to begin with a focus on creating a culture of trust, and a lowering of the psychological risks that are present when one reveals oneself to one's peers.

A simple idea for encouraging greater trust is to begin with activities among teachers that are not perceived as risky. It might be forming a discussion group around an article or book of interest related to an aspect of teaching practice. Teachers can thereby discuss and express their opinions without revealing too much of their own practice. Next, teachers might be encouraged to voluntarily form pairs. One teacher might visit the other's classroom and observe for a period of time. The idea is to have teachers, of their own choosing, make such visits with no judgmental responsibilities, just to watch the dynamics of the class. The teachers would then trade positions and visit their partner's class. Following each visit, they would discuss with each other what they saw. A low-risk assignment would be to pick out positive activities or ideas that one teacher learned from the other. The teachers do not have to be of the same grade or assignment.

Begin with a focus on creating a culture of trust, and a lowering of the psychological risks that are present when one reveals oneself to one's peers.

The aim of this activity is to build a certain level of comfort. If there are a number of pairs, they could switch partners to gain different experiences and differing kinds of feedback. The postobservation discussions eventually should point to particular areas of focus that might emerge from the visits. For example, a teacher might find that his or her partner has developed a very efficient method for managing routine processes such as taking attendance and getting students engaged quickly. Another teacher may have a particular talent for setting up the room environment to motivate and stimulate learning. Another teacher may have discovered how to "reach" a particularly challenging student, which might give the visiting teacher new ideas. The emphasis is to use the positive to build trust and a climate of natural inquiry.

After reaching a certain level of trust, the focus of observation might shift to areas of challenge or frustration. At this point, teachers will be more open to sharing an area of challenge, because they will inevitably begin to realize, as a result of the observations, that *all* teachers face unsolved challenges.

WHAT SHOULD LEARNING COMMUNITIES TALK ABOUT?

The structure of a learning community matters. Who sets the agenda matters. There are no simple answers to these issues. On the question of who sets the agenda, one point of view suggests that the learning community *collectively* sets the agenda. If a particular topic of focus is mandated by someone outside the group, it is doomed to fail, so the argument goes.

Another point of view suggests that, if learning communities are left to their own devices, they will focus on issues that are safe, less risky, inconsequential, and will never tackle issues with a higher payoff for student learning. The fear is that learning communities can evolve into emotional support groups that promote self-esteem but fall short on changing teaching practices that result in greater student learning. This view suggests that the topics should be determined and tied to specific learning goals and objectives developed by the school and district.

One useful framework for determining what learning communities should deal with involves the core propositions and standards of the National Board for Professional Teaching Standards.

A way out of this dilemma is to use aspects of both approaches. That is, a framework can be developed by school and district leadership that lays out a set of values and desirable outcomes. Within this framework, a school learning community can choose to emphasize certain areas, based on an assessment that analyzes their progress against a set of desirable outcomes.

One useful framework for determining what learning communities should deal with involves the core propositions and standards of the National Board for Professional Teaching Standards. The core propositions describe a set of values for teachers upon which standards of practice can be developed. These propositions were written by outstanding practitioners and top researchers over a period of years and represent a professional consensus framework for what teachers should know and be able to do. Within the framework, a learning community can determine a focus for assessing its progress and establish the content for meaningful discussions. In addition, National Board standards for accomplished teaching have been developed for virtually all teaching fields and levels. These standards focus on key areas of practice that are the basis for measuring accomplished teaching. Taken together, they represent a useful way for teachers to assess themselves against a set of values and standards that represent the profession's best effort to define accomplished teaching.

The following points represent a brief explanation of the National Board's Five Core Propositions.

1. Teachers Are Committed to Students and Their Learning

This proposition draws on what we know about knowledge, skills, and dispositions of effective teaching. Effective teachers act on the belief that all students can learn at acceptable levels and make sure that knowledge is accessible to all students. They treat students equitably and adjust instruction accordingly using good professional judgment to make sure all students are engaged and learning to acceptable levels. Effective teachers understand how students learn and develop in a given context and can use best practices to help all students meet stated goals.

2. Teachers Know the Subjects They Teach and How to Teach Those Subjects to Students

Effective teachers have a deep understanding of their subject and understand how their discipline is organized, created, and linked to other disciplines. They possess special knowledge and skill regarding how to engage students with the teaching subject. They are aware of preconceptions and background knowledge that students typically bring to each subject. Their instructional skills allow them to create multiple paths to the subjects they teach.

3. Teachers Are Responsible for Managing Student Learning

Effective teachers command a range of instructional techniques, know when each is important, and can implement them as needed. They know how to organize instruction to meet school goals. They understand how to motivate students and how to maintain their interest. They can assess the progress of individual students as well as the class as a whole. They employ multiple methods for measuring student growth and can explain student performance to parents.

4. Teachers Think Systematically About Their Practice and Learn From Experience

Effective teachers can adopt an experimental and problem-solving orientation to their teaching. They can analyze their instruction, drawing on current knowledge of human development, subject matter, and an understanding of their students to make principled judgments about sound practice. Their decisions are grounded on the latest research, as well as their own professional experience. As lifelong learners, they critically examine their practice—always expanding their skills and sharpening their judgment to adapt their teaching to new research, ideas, and theories.

5. Teachers Are Members of Learning Communities

Effective teachers do not work alone. They realize that their effectiveness is tied to the effectiveness of the school in working collaboratively with other professionals on instructional policy, curriculum development, and teacher development. They can evaluate school progress and the allocation of school resources in relation to local, state, and national education standards. They can knowledgeably deploy school and community resources to benefit their students. Effective teachers understand the value of working collaboratively with parents, and engage productively with them for the benefit of students.

In sum, the core propositions paint images of effective teachers that are multifaceted and complex. The National Board's image of an accomplished teacher recognizes that there are simultaneously science, art, and craft dimensions to the act of teaching. An effective teacher understands that certain research-based practices yield better results than other practices, depending on the context and circumstances. This underscores the notion that teaching is part science, in that there is a growing body of

Effective teachers realize that their effectiveness is tied to the effectiveness of the school in working collaboratively with other professionals on instructional policy, curriculum development, and teacher development.

research identifying particular practices and behaviors that are more effective. The research regarding effective practices in the teaching of reading as well as the cognitive science research about how the brain processes information are examples of the science that supports effective practice.

The artistic dimension of teaching acknowledges that there are different paths to the same outcome. Two teachers may teach the same subject and be equally effective with students, but have widely different styles based on their personalities and their interactive approach with students. Effective teachers use creativity and style in accomplishing similar objectives. An effective teacher understands that students learn in different ways and require different approaches to reach them. Teachers are performers who must engage with their audience (students) in effective ways to produce desirable student outcomes.

Teaching is also a craft that calls for professional judgment. Skilled teachers reflect on their practice for the purpose of evaluating what worked and did not work so that adjustments can be made to be more effective with all students. An effective teacher realizes that every context is different and no two students are exactly alike. To make an analogy, a physician may decide that 10 patients with the same malady may require different treatments. The decision to vary the treatment will depend on a professional judgment that includes the background and circumstances surrounding each patient. Effective teachers operate in the same way, using professional judgment to meet the needs of every student.

The core propositions of the National Board offer a large canvas for determining the work content of the learning community.

The core propositions of the National Board offer a large canvas for determining the work content of the learning community. The experience that teachers go through when they are candidates for National Board Certification provides a way to internalize and operationalize the standards and core propositions. Candidates for National Board Certification spend anywhere from 200 to 400 hours developing a portfolio that requires them to videotape themselves in the classroom in two different contexts. They are also expected to provide samples of student and teacher work that address the relevant standards. Each area of focus requires extensive written analysis of their teaching practice against the established standards. When teachers go through the National Board Certification process with their colleagues in a cohort fashion, they consistently remark about the transformative power of the process that caused them to look at their practice differently. Some teachers—on their own or with the help of a support group—form candidate support "communities" within schools. Others work across schools and communities. Although the motivation is to work toward certification, the vehicle is the formation

question existing practice, where this is warranted. Professional learning communities are *not* families in the sense of the principal being the benevolent but emotionally controlling matriarch or patriarch, while the teachers serve as surrogate children. Interestingly, in the study by James and his colleagues of the 10 highly effective Welsh schools, educators did *not* refer to their schools as families— since, as James points out, mature cultures do not replay or replace the hierarchical emotional dependencies of family life within official school settings.

In strong and sustainable professional communities, improvement is evident throughout the life and learning of the school, across a broad and enriching curriculum, in fulfilling relationships as well as earnest performance, and in an empowered environment of grown-up norms where people can challenge one another, manage up as well as manage down, and where confident principals and superintendents can encourage as well as endure all of this as everyone strives to find the strategies and solutions that can support improved learning and increased achievement among all students.

6. Inclusive and Responsive Communities

In January 2007, with team colleagues Gabor Halasz and Beatriz Pont, I undertook an investigative inquiry for the Organisation for Economic Co-operation and Development (OECD) into the relationship between leadership and school improvement in one of the world's highest-performing educational systems and economies: Finland. After we visited and interviewed students, teachers, head teachers, system administrators, university researchers, and senior ministry officials, a remarkably unified narrative began to surface about the country, its schools, and their sense of aspiration, struggle, and destiny.

Finland is a nation that has endured almost seven centuries of domination and oppression—achieving true independence only within the last three generations. In the context of this historical legacy, and in the face of a harsh and demanding climate and northern geography, it is not surprising that one of the most popular Finnish sayings translates as "It was long, and it was hard, but we did it!"

Yet it is not simply stoic perseverance, fed by a Lutheran ethic of hard work and resilience, that explains Finland's success as a high-performing educational system and economy. At the core of this country's success and sustainability is its capacity to reconcile, harmonize, and integrate those elements that have divided other developed economies and societies—a prosperous, high-performing economy and a decent, socially just society. While the knowledge economy has weakened the welfare state in many other societies, in Finland a strong welfare state is a central part of the national narrative that supports and sustains a successful economy.

In *The Information Society and the Welfare State,* Castells and Himanen (2002) describe how

> Finland shows that a fully fledged welfare state is not incompatible with technological innovation, with the development of the information society, and with a dynamic, competitive new economy. Indeed, it appears to be a decisive contributing factor to the growth of this new economy on a stable basis. (p. 166)

The contrast with Anglo-Saxon countries where material wealth has been gained at the expense of increasing social division, and also at the cost of children's well-being (UNICEF, 2007), could not be more striking.

> Finland stands in sharp contrast to the Silicon Valley model that is entirely driven by market mechanisms, individual entrepreneurialism, and the culture of risk—with considerable social costs, acute social inequality, and a deteriorating basis for both locally generated human capital and economic infrastructure. (Castells & Himanen, 2002, p. 167)

At the center of this successful integration that, in less than half a century, has transformed Finland from a rural backwater country into a high-tech economic powerhouse is the country's educational system. As the respondents interviewed by the OECD team indicated at all levels, Finns are driven by a common and articulately expressed social vision that connects a creative and prosperous future—as epitomized by the Nokia telecommunications company, whose operations and suppliers account for about 40% of the country's GDP (Haikio, 2002)—to the people's sense of themselves as having a creative history and social identity. One of the schools we visited was just 2 miles from the home of Finland's iconic classical composer Jean Sibelius. The visual, creative, and performing arts are an integral part of Finnish children's education and lifelong learning all through and even beyond their secondary school experience.

Technological creativity and competitiveness, therefore, do not break Finns from their past but instead connect them to it in a unitary narrative of lifelong learning and societal development. All this occurs within a strong welfare state that supports and steers (a favorite word in Finland) the educational system and the economy. A strong public system of education provides education free of charge as a universal right all the way through public school and higher education—including all necessary resources, equipment, musical instruments, and free school meals for everyone. Science and technology are high priorities, though not at the expense of the arts and creativity. Almost 3% of the nation's GDP is allocated to scientific and technological development; a national committee that includes leading corporate executives and university presidents, and that is chaired by the prime minister, steers and integrates economic and educational strategy.

As Finnish commentators and analysts have also remarked, all of this educational and economic integration occurs within a society that values children, education, and social welfare; that has high regard for education and educators as servants of the public good; that ranks teaching as the most desired occupation of high school graduates; and that is therefore able to make entry into teaching demanding and highly competitive (Aho, Pitkanen, & Sahlberg, 2006; Sahlberg, 2006).

Within a generally understood social vision, the state steers but does not prescribe in detail the national curriculum—with trusted teams of highly qualified teachers writing the detailed curriculum together at the level of the municipality, in ways that adjust to the students whom they know best. In schools that are characterized by an uncanny calmness, teachers exercise their palpable sense of professional and social responsibility in their efforts to care especially for children at the bottom, so as to lift them to the level of the rest. This is achieved not by endless initiatives or targeted interventions but by quiet cooperation (another favorite word) among all the teachers involved.

Principals in Finland are required by law to have been teachers themselves; most continue to be engaged in classroom teaching for at least 2 to 3 hours per week—which lends them credibility among their teachers; enables them to remain connected to their children; and ensures that pedagogical leadership is not merely high-flown rhetoric but is a living, day-to-day reality. According to one interviewee in the OECD study, the reason that principals say they are able to do all of this without being overloaded is because, "unlike the Anglo-Saxon countries, [they] do not have to spend time responding to long lists of government initiatives that come from the top."

Finland contains essential lessons for societies that aspire, educationally and economically, to be successful, as well as for sustainable creative knowledge societies and schools that want to behave more like professional learning communities. Building a future without completely breaking from the past; supporting not only pedagogical change but also continuity; fostering strong connections between education and economic skills development without sacrifice to culture and creativity; raising standards by lifting the many rather than pushing a privileged few; connecting private goals to the public good; developing a highly qualified and regarded profession that brings about improvement through trust, cooperation, and responsibility; embedding and embodying instructional leadership into almost every principal's weekly activity; and emphasizing principles of professional and community-based rather than merely managerial accountability—these are just some of the essential lessons to be taken from Finland's exceptional educational and economic journey.

Finland contains essential lessons for societies that aspire, educationally and economically, to be successful, as well as for sustainable creative knowledge societies and schools that want to behave more like professional learning communities.

Yet it is important to acknowledge that Finland's integration of the information economy and the welfare state as a continuous narrative of legacy and progress that defines the national identity is not without its blind spots. Having been an embattled and oppressed historical minority, Finland remains a somewhat xenophobic society, suspicious of immigrants and outsiders, and threatened by those who challenge or diverge from the Finnish way of life (Castells & Himanen, 2002). Without a willingness to accommodate higher rates of immigration, the impending retirement of large proportions of Baby Boomer employees (as many municipal administrators described it to us) will also increase the financial burden on the welfare state and jeopardize the basic sustainability of Finland's economy and society that depends on it.

The onset of such diversity may require strategies of inclusiveness not yet embraced by the Finns. Objective data may be required to pick up the early warning signs of difficulty from students whose responses are culturally different—and Finland's long-standing opposition to international testing may need to loosen somewhat as a result. Other kinds of students within Finland and beyond may also benefit from different teaching methods and strategies that are more culturally responsive and appropriate—meshing more closely with the cultural knowledge and learning styles that children bring with them to school (Delpit, 1995; Ladson-Billings, 1995).

Taking the cue from Finland but also thinking beyond it, inclusive and responsive communities care about and serve their diverse students in ways that make sense and work for them culturally; they recruit, retain, and engage highly qualified teachers who thrive on the empowerment, discretion, and support that are at the heart of professionalism; they are sustained by deeply held ethics of trust, collaboration, and responsibility; and they are part of a great social vision where commitment to the public good, as evidenced in private sacrifice and redistributive taxation, is principled and strong.

7. Activist and Empowered Communities

But what is to be done when the wealthiest nation in the world resists increasing taxation to fund the public educational good and argues instead only for reallocating existing resources (National Center on Education and the Economy, 2007); when it languishes next to last out of 22 industrialized countries on international indicators of child well-being (UNICEF, 2007); when it refuses to provide adequate health or welfare support for its poorest children (Berliner, 2006); and when even literacy materials and decent books, never mind food or musical instruments, often have to be provided through charitable donations for the country's poorest communities?

It is helpful here to move from Finland in the far north to the edgy streets of culturally diverse Los Angeles to find a stronger test of how professional learning communities might need to become more socially inclusive and activist communities, if they are to create the shake-up in society and bureaucracy that is necessary for lifting up their students and their schools.

Jeannie Oakes and her colleagues at the University of California, Los Angeles, argue that conventional change and reform strategies fail because the learning and teaching envisaged does not have clearly articulated goals concerning social justice other than those narrowly concerned with tested achievement and achievement gaps (Oakes, Rogers, & Lipton, 2006). Moreover, the strategies for bringing about change are directed at and driven by school and school system professionals; students and parents are rarely involved other than as targets for or consumers of the change effort. In this sense, neither the means nor the ends of most change efforts—nor the theories of action that underpin them—challenge or confront the structures of power and control in society that systematically protect the schools, programs, and instructional strategies that are especially advantageous for white elites and their children.

In response, Oakes and colleagues (2006) draw on John Dewey's principles of participative inquiry as well as American traditions of community activism and organizing to propose classroom and school-level changes that raise achievement and secure wider improvement by connecting low-achieving poor and minority students to university researchers and teacher inquiry networks that train and support them to inquire into, and then act upon, the conditions of their own education and lives. Such forms of collaborative inquiry are not merely culturally responsive pedagogies that respond to the culturally variable learning styles of diverse students, nor are they simply acts of cooperative instruction or intellectual creativity that enhance cognitive achievement. Rather, in line with the legacy of Paulo Freire (2000), these practices, which Oakes and colleagues help to create in practice as well as in theory, increase achievement and improve the conditions for other people's achievement by helping students inquire into, understand, and want to act on the conditions that affect the lives and education of themselves and their communities—dilapidated buildings, large class sizes, divisive tracking practices, inadequate books and materials, shortages of qualified teachers, and restricted opportunities to learn.

In the end, the strongest professional learning communities in a nation that appears to have abandoned its poorest children are inclusive, empowered, and activist communities that bring professionals, parents, and others together.

These pedagogically transformative practices are linked to an activist orientation among involved students and also among those parents and local communities who relentlessly challenge bureaucrats and legislators with evidence-based arguments as well

as disruptive strategies and knowledge, with the aim of providing gen-
uinely equal opportunities for the poor alongside the affluent.

These living "pedagogies of the oppressed" may not be able to be
scaled up everywhere—especially beyond the large urban centers where
local research and philanthropic capacity are strong, an objection
that Oakes et al. (2006) sweep aside far too easily—but networks of
advocacy for publicly driven, rather than bureaucratically imposed,
reform are spreading rapidly across America (Shirley & Evans, in
press), with activist pedagogies of inquiry among parents and
students alike being a fundamental factor in this growing area of
influence. In the end, the strongest professional learning communities in a nation that appears to have abandoned its poorest children
are inclusive, empowered, and activist communities that bring professionals, parents, and others together to make the commitments,
create the conditions, and develop the capacity that enable their children to succeed—and that hold governments and bureaucracies
accountable for making this happen.

In these circumstances, school principals and superintendents
are not just building managers or even instructional leaders; they
are leaders of their students, their fellow professionals, their wider
communities—and indeed of their societies as a whole in collective
pursuit of a greater social good as professionals, community workers, and citizens.

CONCLUSION

This chapter has set out seven images of professional learning communities. So much of what passes for professional learning communities amounts to a corruption of their fundamental principles and
purposes—being little more than a change in title, a hyperactive
diversion, an autistic obsession with numbers and targets, or a pre-
text for insisting on compliance and imposing control.

It is up to all of us to make certain that professional learning communities do not degenerate into new forms of domination or distraction, but that they become and remain all that their creators intended
for them: places of collaboration, learning, community, and hope,
where professionals, parents, and community members strive and
struggle to ensure that their schools and all their students are the best
they can be.

REFERENCES

Achinstein, B., & Ogawa, R. (2006). (In)Fidelity: What the resistance of new teachers reveals about professional principles and prescriptive educational policies. *Harvard Educational Review, 76*(1), 30–63.

Aho, E., Pitkanen, K., & Sahlberg, P. (2006). *Policy development and reform principles of basic and secondary education in Finland since 1968.* Washington, DC: World Bank.

Berliner, D. (2006). Our impoverished view of educational reform. *Teachers College Record, 108*(6), 949–995.

Campbell, E. (2005). Challenges in fostering ethical knowledge as professionalism within schools as teaching communities. *Journal of Educational Change, 6*(3), 207–226.

Castells, M., & Himanen, P. (2002). *The information society and the welfare state: The Finnish model.* Oxford, UK: Oxford University Press.

Delpit, L. (1995). *Other people's children.* New York: The New Press.

Dodd, D., & Favaro, K. (2007). *The three tensions.* San Francisco: Jossey-Bass.

DuFour, R. E., & Eaker, R. (1998). *Professional learning communities at work: Best practices for enhancing student achievement.* Bloomington, IN: National Educational Service.

Eaker, R., DuFour, R., & Burnette, R. (2002). *Getting started: Reculturing schools to become professional learning communities.* Bloomington, IN: National Educational Service.

Foucault, M. (1977). *Discipline and punish: The birth of the prison.* New York: Pantheon.

Freire, P. (2000). *Pedagogy of the oppressed.* London: Continuum International.

Fullan, M. (2007). *Turnaround leadership.* San Francisco: Jossey-Bass.

Giles, C., & Hargreaves, A. (2006). The sustainability of innovative schools as learning organizations and professional learning communities during standardized reform. *Educational Administration Quarterly, 42*(1), 124–156.

Haikio, M. (2002). *Nokia: The inside story.* Helsinki, Finland: Edita.

Hargreaves, A. (2003). *Teaching in the knowledge society: Education in the age of insecurity.* New York: Teachers College Press.

Hargreaves, A., Shirley, D., Evans, M., Johnson, C., & Riseman, D. (2006). *The long and the short of raising achievement: Final report of the evaluation of the "Raising Achievement, Transforming Learning" project of the UK Specialist Schools and Academies Trust.* Chestnut Hill, MA: Boston College.

James, C., Connolly, M., Dunning, G., & Elliott, T. (2006). *How very effective primary schools work.* London: Sage.

Ladson-Billings, G. (1995). Toward a theory of culturally relevant peda-gogy. *American Educational Research Journal, 33*(3), 465–492.

McKibben, B. (2007). *Deep economy: The wealth of communities and the durable future.* New York: Times Books.

McLaughlin, M., & Mitra, D. (2003). *The cycle of inquiry as the engine of school reform: Lessons from the Bay Area School Reform Collaborative.* Stanford, CA: Center for Research on the Context of Teaching.

McLaughlin, M. W., & Talbert, J. E. (2006). *Building school-based teacher learning communities: Professional strategies to improve student achievement.* New York: Teachers College Press.

National Center on Education and the Economy. (2007). *Tough choices or tough times: The report of the New Commission on the Skills of the American Workforce.* San Francisco: Wiley.

Naylor, C. (2005). *A teacher union's collaborative research agenda and strategies: One way forward for Canadian teacher unions in supporting teachers' professional development.* Vancouver, Canada: British Columbia Teachers' Federation.

Oakes, J., Rogers, J., & Lipton, M. (2006). *Learning power: Organizing for education and justice.* New York: Teachers College Press.

Sahlberg, P. (2006). Education reform for raising economic competitiveness. *Journal of Educational Change, 7*(4), 259–287.

Sanchez, M. (2006). *Teachers' experiences implementing English-only legislation.* Unpublished doctoral dissertation, Boston College, Chestnut Hill, MA.

Sennett, R. (1998). *The corrosion of character: The personal consequences of work in the new capitalism.* London: Norton.

Shirley, D., & Evans, M. (in press). Community organizing and No Child Left Behind. In M. Orr (Ed.), *The ecology of civic engagement.* Lawrence: University Press of Kansas.

UNICEF. (2007). Child poverty in perspective: An overview of child well-being in rich countries. *Innocenti Report Card* 7. Florence, Italy: Innocenti Research Centre. Available online at http://www.unicef.org/media/files/ChildPovertyReport.pdf.

Wilson, B. (1961). *Sects and society: The sociology of three religious groups in Britain.* London: Heinemann.

INDEX

Page numbers in italics indicate figures or tables.

social and emotional learning, 62–63,
65–66, 69, *92–93,* 134–35
Inclusive and responsive communities,
189–93
Information. *See* Data
*Information Society and the Welfare
State, The,* 190
Internal accountability, 134–35
Interventions, pyramid of, 12

James, C., 189
Job enlargement, PLCs as, 46

Kilgore, Ashby, 11, 20

Lateral accountability, 17–20
Leacock, E. B., 165
Leadership
characteristics of, 164–65, 191–92
collaborative learning communities,
161–70
distributed, 133–34
PLC, 26, 35, 48–49, 195
SEL, 101–3, 105, 125
support for PLC, 157–58
teams, 101–3
transformation of, 165–67
Leading in a Culture of Change, 16
Learning communities. *See* Professional
learning communities (PLCs)
Lieberman, Ann, 157
Limited-English speakers, 9
Literacy, standards-based, 131–33
Lives of Others, The, 180
Longevity standards, 140
Louis, Karen S., 43

Marks, Helen, 43
Maxwell, John, 161
McLaughlin, M., 182
Membership in PLCs, 26, 29–30,
151–53, 188–89
governance of, 32–33
organization of, 30–32
Mentoring, 13–14, 14–15
Mid-year reflection, 114–15
Minority students, 9, 122–23,
154, 193–94

Mitra, D., 182
Motivation and readiness for SELs,
68–69, 88, 89, *90–92*
Multisite SELs, 63–66

National Board Certified Teachers,
143–44, 152–53
National Board for Professional
Teaching Standards, 143, 149–53,
157–58
National Staff Development Council, 171
Naylor, Charles, 176
Networking and integration of
staff, 53–54, 183–84
New York Times, 144
Newport News Education Association, 11
Newport News Educational
Foundation, 11
Newport News, Virginia
building on strengths, 7
building trust, relationships,
and the team, 8–9, 14–15
celebrating successes, 10
clarifying and crystallizing the
vision, 7
clarity of intent, 10–11
communicating the vision, 7–8
creating a pathway to success, 9
disparity between students in, 5
district background and overview, 6
lateral accountability, 17–20
school accreditation, 6
vision, 7
Newsome, Marcus, 6–11, 20
No Child Left Behind, 6
Nokia, 190
Nonsustained SEL sites, 87–89

Oakes, Jeannie, 193, 195
OECD. *See* Organisation for Economic
Co-operation and Development
(OECD)
Oliver, Kimberly, 153–54
Open Circle Social Competency
Program, 98, 100
Organisation for Economic Co-operation
and Development (OECD), 189, 190
Organizational learning, 50–52

CORWIN
PRESS

The Corwin Press logo—a raven striding across an open book—represents the union of courage and learning. Corwin Press is committed to improving education for all learners by publishing books and other professional development resources for those serving the field of PreK–12 education. By providing practical, hands-on materials, Corwin Press continues to carry out the promise of its motto: **"Helping Educators Do Their Work Better."**

The HOPE Foundation logo stands for Harnessing Optimism and Potential Through Education. The HOPE Foundation helps to develop and support educational leaders over time at district- and statewide levels to create school cultures that sustain all students' achievement, especially low-performing students.

American Association of
School Administrators

The American Association of School Administrators, founded in 1865, is the professional organization for over 13,000 educational leaders across America and in many other countries. AASA's mission is to support and develop effective school system leaders who are dedicated to the highest quality public education for all children.